To:

From:

Date:

Carey Scott

PRAY
& NEVER
GIVE UP

Devotions and Prayers for Women

BARBOUR
PUBLISHING

Published by Barbour Publishing, Inc., 1810 Barbour Drive, Uhrichsville, Ohio 44683, www.barbourbooks.com

Our mission is to inspire the world with the life-changing message of the Bible.

 Member of the
Evangelical Christian
Publishers Association

Printed in China.

PRAY &
BE BLESSED!

Prayer is a conversation you have with God, and it delights His heart when you make it a priority each day. There is nothing too simple or boring, nothing too heavy or cumbersome to share with Him. You don't need the perfect words or phrasing to impress God. There's no specific time or place that enhances the quality or effectiveness of your prayers. And you don't need to have it all together before you approach His throne. Friend, the Lord just wants to hear from you.

Let your prayers be honest expressions about what you're feeling. Be transparent about the burdens you're carrying and the hopes you're clinging to. Unpack your fears and insecurities. Share each victory, including all the glorious details. Tell God what you need from Him, because He is listening. And when you pray and don't give up, something beautiful comes from it. Because you have opened up to the Lord, you will be primed to see blessings flow.

The devotions in this book will start you on your adventure of prayer with God. If you let them, they will be a daily encouragement to talk to Him about anything and everything. And you will be blessed in meaningful and extraordinary ways!

SATURATED IN PRAYER

Don't be pulled in different directions or worried about a thing.
Be saturated in prayer throughout each day, offering your
faith-filled requests before God with overflowing gratitude.
Tell him every detail of your life, then God's wonderful
peace that transcends human understanding,
will guard your heart and mind through Jesus Christ.

PHILIPPIANS 4:6–7 TPT

When you choose to saturate yourself in prayer, talking to God throughout the day, you'll experience peace that others can't begin to understand. If in those moments when life gets hairy you take a moment to talk to the Lord about the emotions swirling in your anxious heart, a sense of calm will prevail. The problem is that life pulls us in a million different directions, and most of them are unsettling at best. We battle with insecurities that tangle us from the inside out, keeping us stirred up and unable to think clearly. And our minds go down paths where the outcomes are usually terrible and tragic. That anxiety should lead us right to the feet of God, looking for His hand to soothe us and restore what worry has taken away. Don't waste a moment trying to fix things yourself. Go right to God in faith and let Him bless you.

Father in heaven, I'm desperate for the kind of peace
only You can provide. I'm overwhelmed and
under water and asking You to bless me with Your
presence. In the name of Jesus I pray. Amen.

CONTINUOUS PRAYER

*Keep your thoughts continually fixed on all that is authentic
and real, honorable and admirable, beautiful and respectful,
pure and holy, merciful and kind. And fasten your thoughts
on every glorious work of God, praising him always. Put into
practice the example of all that you have heard from me or seen
in my life and the God of peace will be with you in all things.*

PHILIPPIANS 4:8–9 TPT

The idea is that we praise God continually. If all good things come
from Him, then He should get credit for everything good. Whatever
is authentic, honorable, beautiful, pure, and kind points back to God.
What is real, admirable, respectful, holy, and merciful is a reflection
of His goodness. Your gratitude should weave its way through your
day. Let it be a fluid conversation that ends when you close your eyes
at night. Your mind should be focused on seeing His hand in your
life. And your heart should be collecting those beautiful moments of
blessing so you don't forget how much you are loved.

**Father in heaven, I see Your goodness in my life. Help
me notice every good thing and give You the glory for it.
You're simply amazing in every way, and I'm blessed by
how You love me. In the name of Jesus I pray. Amen.**

PRAY FOR ABSOLUTELY EVERYTHING

Jesus was matter-of-fact: "Embrace this God-life. Really embrace it, and nothing will be too much for you. This mountain, for instance: Just say, 'Go jump in the lake'—no shuffling or hemming and hawing— and it's as good as done. That's why I urge you to pray for absolutely everything, ranging from small to large. Include everything as you embrace this God-life, and you'll get God's everything. And when you assume the posture of prayer, remember that it's not all asking."
MARK 11:22–25 MSG

You have the freedom to pray for whatever it is you want or need. When you talk to God, He invites you to ask without fear and without insecurity. You can talk to Him about anything and everything. Big or small, God wants you to bring it to the throne room and share it with heartfelt authenticity. Are you worried you won't find the right job? Do you struggle with how to best raise your kids in today's culture? Are you lonely and unsure if you'll ever find companionship? Are the signs of aging beginning to take their toll on your self-worth? Do you need to defeat the Goliath in front of you? No matter what's going on in your life, God wants in on it. And it's His power through your prayers that brings hope and healing to a defeated soul in need of restoration.

Father in heaven, You know the reasons my heart is heavy. I need Your help. In the name of Jesus I pray. Amen.

HE GIVES AND TAKES AWAY

*I was naked, with nothing, when I came from my
mother's womb; and naked, with nothing, I will return
to the earth. The Eternal has given, and He has taken
away. May the name of the Eternal One be blessed.*

JOB 1:21 VOICE

When we understand that God is the one who gives and takes away according to His will, it will change the way we pray. It will give us a better understanding of His omnipotence. We will bow to His all-powerfulness. We'll realize God is the one in control, and it will be a source of peace. It will allow us to exhale as we surrender to His authority. And while we certainly have the gift of free will, it doesn't negate God's sovereignty. Tell Him how this truth blesses you and why you're grateful His hands are deep in the soil of your life. Your choices may be why something is lost or gained, but He knew it would be and will use it for your benefit. Friend, let your heart rest, and trust that God's got you in His hand today and always. Nothing that happens catches Him off guard.

**Father in heaven, it blesses me to know You're in
control. I'm grateful You have the insight to give and
take away so I benefit in the end. Help me keep the right
perspective on this powerful truth, even when I may
not understand. In the name of Jesus I pray. Amen.**

GOD'S WORDS AT HOME IN YOU

*"But if you make yourselves at home with me and my
words are at home in you, you can be sure that whatever
you ask will be listened to and acted upon."*

JOHN 15:7 MSG

The Lord wants to bless your requests, but only when they are aligned
with His will for your life. Sometimes people read today's verse and
are frustrated when the new and improved husband isn't who walks
in the door after work. They're angry when money isn't pouring in
like they requested. When the cancer doesn't immediately disappear,
some walk away from their faith. They give up on God when pregnancy
continues to elude them. But when the Lord's words *are at home* in
us, it means we understand that His will and ways are above ours.
In faith, we choose to trust them over our own. And when we do, our
language in prayer will reflect it. We will share our hopes and dreams
with God, ending with "But Your will be done, not mine." God hears
your heart and has plans already in place to bless you with the right
answer at the right time.

**Father in heaven, let my requests reflect my faith in You. Let
Your words be on my tongue so I am asking in alignment with
Your will and ways. I know You hear my prayers, and I want Your
blessing to abound in my life. In the name of Jesus I pray. Amen.**

MAKE YOUR LIFE A PRAYER

Let joy be your continual feast. Make your life a prayer.
And in the midst of everything be always giving thanks,
for this is God's perfect plan for you in Christ Jesus.

1 THESSALONIANS 5:16–18 TPT

How do you make your life a prayer? What changes need to happen so every day is a beautiful connection between you and God? Maybe a good start would be to make sure your words and actions point to Him. It would help to cultivate a grateful attitude, the ability to recognize the amazing ways the Lord has blessed you in the midst of your mess. Pursuing joy in the good and the bad times would also be key. But it would also require a surrendered heart to God, acknowledging Him as King of your life. When you put forth the effort to make your life a prayer, you will be blessed in meaningful ways. It may not secure you a perfect or easy experience on earth, but your life will be full of purpose. You will have lived with passion. And your story will be an encouragement to others for years to come.

Father in heaven, help me be intentional to make my life a prayer to You. Give me the courage to follow You more than what my flesh desires. And let everything I do and all that I say reflect my faithful heart for You. In the name of Jesus I pray. Amen.

DON'T ROLE-PLAY IN PRAYER

"Here's what I want you to do: Find a quiet, secluded place so you won't be tempted to role-play before God. Just be there as simply and honestly as you can manage. The focus will shift from you to God, and you will begin to sense his grace."

MATTHEW 6:6 MSG

When we know others are watching or listening, our prayers can sometimes become a performance. We may end up talking to God out loud in hopes that we sound holy or elevated. We may try to use big, flowery words to impress. And we may even try to bring in scripture as a way to amaze the Lord or sound important to those listening. Maybe that's why scripture tells us to pray in places where we won't be tempted to role-play. God always wants your authentic self—the self who opens up with honesty about what's on your heart. Too often, we complicate what should be simple about prayer. So make sure the focus is off you and on God. Talk to Him from a place of humility, and you'll sense His grace and delight immediately.

Father in heaven, keep me from trying to impress anyone as I pray. I don't need my prayers to be applauded by others. Instead, let my heart be revealed to You alone in honest moments together. I want the blessings that come from living an authentic life in Your presence. In the name of Jesus I pray. Amen.

BEING PRESENT IN PRAYER

*"When you pray, there is no need to repeat empty phrases,
praying like the Gentiles do, for they expect God to hear them
because of their many words. There is no need to imitate them,
since your Father already knows what you need before you ask him."*
MATTHEW 6:7–8 TPT

Today's scripture offers us a great challenge to be present in prayer. It's reminding us to be meaningful and intentional. Think about it. Do you ever find yourself praying the same statements over and over again? It's not that there's anything wrong with repetitive prayer. We just have to guard against empty words. Just saying the words out of habit reveals a disconnect, making the prayer more of a form prayer than a heartfelt one. Are you present in your prayers? Are you connecting your heart to God's as you talk to Him? That time with the Lord will bless you deeply if you stay in the moment and speak from authentic places.

Father in heaven, I confess there are times I pray the right words without feeling them. I get stuck in a rut of using the same phrases and statements over and over. You already know what's on my heart. Help me connect to Your heart as I share my concerns. In the name of Jesus I pray. Amen.

THE HOLY SPIRIT RISES UP

And in a similar way, the Holy Spirit takes hold of us in our human frailty to empower us in our weakness. For example, at times we don't even know how to pray, or know the best things to ask for. But the Holy Spirit rises up within us to super-intercede on our behalf, pleading to God with emotional sighs too deep for words.

ROMANS 8:26 TPT

There are times we just don't have the words. Maybe it's because we're not sure what we're really thinking or feeling. Maybe we can't let ourselves speak our thoughts or feelings out loud because it will make everything feel real. Maybe the only sound we can muster is a guttural cry from deep inside. The reality is there are moments when our humanity gets the best of us, and we're left feeling weak. But the blessing in prayer comes from knowing that the Holy Spirit, who resides in our hearts, empowers us. Scripture says He "rises up within us" to intercede on our behalf. He is the one who talks to God in the deepest of ways—a way that is crystal clear between them. A way we're unable to match.

Father in heaven, thank You for the blessing of the Holy Spirit interceding for me in prayer. It's a relief to know that when I don't have the words to share, He will make sure the message gets to You. In the name of Jesus I pray. Amen.

PRAYER ISN'T A THEATRICAL PRODUCTION

"And when you come before God, don't turn that into a theatrical production either. All these people making a regular show out of their prayers, hoping for fifteen minutes of fame! Do you think God sits in a box seat?"

MATTHEW 6:5 MSG

Your prayer life is a sacred space between you and the Lord, a special time of connection that isn't always for public consumption. It's a blessing that comes from recognizing Him as your personal Savior. It's a chance to unpack the deepest contents of your heart with the one who has all the answers. Yes, there are times we pray in a group setting, and it's completely appropriate to pray as a community. But be careful not to let prayer become a performance. Settle yourself into the moment without making it a theatrical production, because God isn't impressed by those motives. When you pray, speak to Him from the heart rather than use words to astound others. Prayer is a holy experience. Whether in private or in public, always be reverent in prayer.

Father in heaven, thank You for the blessing of prayer! What a privilege to speak directly to You anytime I want to or need to. Help me remember that prayer is consecrated and to make my prayers authentic and honest. Keep me from trying to impress You with them. In the name of Jesus I pray. Amen.

WHEN YOU LIVE BY HIS PLAN

*Don't you know that He who pursues and explores the human
heart intimately knows the Spirit's mind because He pleads
to God for His saints to align their lives with the will of God?
We are confident that God is able to orchestrate everything to
work toward something good and beautiful when we love Him
and accept His invitation to live according to His plan.*

ROMANS 8:27–28 VOICE

When you ask the Lord to help you live out His plan for your life, heaven celebrates. A woman who embraces her purpose brings delight to the heart of God. And it's that sweet surrender and deliberate decision to align her life with His that unlocks blessing, the blessing of God's intention to orchestrate everything in her life for good. Good or bad, He will bring beauty. That means the Lord can recycle a divorce, a bankruptcy, a season of sinning, a moral failure, or a bad parenting moment. You're not disqualified. So pray for the courage to walk out God's will for your life with purpose and passion. Ask Him for the confidence to live according to His plan.

Father in heaven, I can't do this without Your help because my humanity limits me. I accept Your invitation, so now please bless me with the supernatural strength and wisdom to follow Your path every chance I get. In the name of Jesus I pray. Amen.

JESUS PLEADS FOR YOU

Who has the authority to condemn? Jesus the Anointed who died,
but more importantly, conquered death when He was raised to
sit at the right hand of God where He pleads on our behalf.

ROMANS 8:34 VOICE

It's hard to imagine that the God who created the heavens and the earth and everything in them cares enough about us to sit and listen to His Son plead on our behalf. At the same time, it's unbelievable that the Jesus who stepped out of heaven to become man, died on a cross for our sins, and rose again after three days is the same Jesus who leans over to the Father and mentions our names. But scripture says it's true. We know the Bible is complete truth, so we accept the blessing with a full heart. You have been part of the plan from the very beginning. Your name has been on God's heart forever, even before He formed something out of nothing. He watched you take shape in your mother's womb. And just because Jesus pleads on your behalf doesn't mean the Lord isn't delighted to hear you share what's on your heart too.

Father in heaven, to know the Godhead cares so much
for me speaks volumes of value into my heart. Thanks
for all the ways I see Your love for me. It doesn't go
unnoticed. In the name of Jesus I pray. Amen.

WHERE DIVORCE CAN'T HAPPEN

Who could ever divorce us from the endless love of God's Anointed One? Absolutely no one! For nothing in the universe has the power to diminish his love toward us. Troubles, pressures, and problems are unable to come between us and heaven's love. What about persecutions, deprivations, dangers, and death threats? No, for they are all impotent to hinder omnipotent love.

ROMANS 8:35 TPT

What a blessing to realize the depth of love God has for us. The powerful reality is there's nothing and no one that could ever persuade the Lord to walk away from us. While people find reasons to divorce themselves from us all the time, there will never be a valid enough reason for Him. We matter too much to God. He can't love you any more or less than He does in this very moment. No problems or pressures can change that truth. Ask the Lord to let that blessing sink deep into the marrow of your bones. It will bring freedom to know you're secure. It will provide peace to realize God's love is unchangeable. And it will exchange your stress for His comfort. Pray for His presence and let it bless you.

Father in heaven, I am relieved to know Your love for me is unmovable and our relationship is unending. I really needed to know that today. In the name of Jesus I pray. Amen.

THEY ARE INCOMPARABLE

*So now I live with the confidence that there is nothing in
the universe with the power to separate us from God's love.
I'm convinced that his love will triumph over death, life's troubles,
fallen angels, or dark rulers in the heavens. There is nothing in
our present or future circumstances that can weaken his love.*

ROMANS 8:38 TPT

Many of us carry the wounds of love that didn't work out. We know
what abandonment feels like on a cellular level. We've faced rejection
too many times to count. And out of that came epic trust issues we
can't seem to overcome and insecurities that keep us too afraid to
try again. Friend, life has a way of punching us in the gut repeatedly,
which is why it's so important we grab on to the truth that earthly
love and godly love are completely different. They are incomparable.
So ask the Lord to open your eyes to see, and He'll bless you with
the knowledge of truth. There are many factors that affect the love
we feel toward others, but nothing in heaven or on earth can weaken
the love God has for us. It will always triumph over everything else.
And in that you can be confident.

**Father in heaven, bless me with the understanding of how
different Your unfailing love is compared to the failed love
the world offers. In the name of Jesus I pray. Amen.**

THE ANSWER IS ALWAYS PRAYER

Are any in your community suffering? They should pray. Are any celebrating? They should sing praises to God. Are any sick? They should call the elders of your church and ask them to pray. They will gather around and anoint them with oil in the name of the Lord.

JAMES 5:13–14 VOICE

No matter what is happening in your life right now—good or not so good—the answer is always to pray. If you're struggling in your marriage, pray for wisdom. If you are grieving the loss of a parent, pray for comfort. If your child passed a math test after studying hard, share a prayer of thanksgiving. If your seasonal allergies are getting the best of you, pray for immediate relief. If your annual review came with an unexpected raise in salary, praise God for provision. If you're feeling alone, pray for community. Prayer is hands down the most powerful weapon in your arsenal because it provides you direct access and constant communication with God. And from it flows abundant blessings as the Lord responds, meeting every need and celebrating each victory.

Father in heaven, what a relief to know I can pray to You no matter what comes my way, be it happy celebrations or hard challenges. Thank You for making a way to talk directly to You. It's my privilege to share my ups and downs with You. In the name of Jesus I pray. Amen.

OWNING UP TO SIN

So own up to your sins to one another and pray for one another. In the end, you may be healed. Your prayers are powerful when they are rooted in a righteous life.

JAMES 5:16 VOICE

It's hard to own up to the things we've done wrong. No one really likes to admit they have failed or fallen short. We don't want to suffer the natural consequences, so we keep our mouths shut and hope it just goes away. But scripture highlights the importance of disclosing our sins to others, and for good reason. God knows how much the Enemy loves to gain a foothold in our lives. If there is unrepented sin, it provides the perfect opportunity for him to grab on. Hidden sin sets us up for the Enemy's trap. But when we reveal, we can heal. Pray that God gives you courage to come clean, but also invite Him to search your heart for unseen sin. Ask for the blessing of healing and restoration. It may be hard to confess when you've messed up, but nothing compares to the freedom it brings.

Father in heaven, I confess I've fallen short of Your glory so many times. Thank You for the blessing of Jesus and His finished work on the cross. Please give me the courage to admit my failures to those I've offended. I don't want to give the Enemy any foothold in my life. In the name of Jesus I pray. Amen.

BE A PERSISTENT PERSON

"So it is with your prayers. Ask and you'll receive. Seek and you'll discover. Knock on heaven's door, and it will one day open for you. Every persistent person will receive what he asks for. Every persistent seeker will discover what he needs. And everyone who knocks persistently will one day find an open door."

LUKE 11:9–10 TPT

When God says something, take heed. When He mentions it again, take another look. But when the Lord brings it up a third time, tattoo it on your heart. In today's scripture alone, we're told three times to be persistent in prayer. Each time, what comes next is the blessing we receive for having that kind of determination. We're told our tenacity will give us what we're asking for. It will enable us to discover what we need. And when we pray with persistence, eventually we will see the right door open at the right time. We simply must exhibit endurance as we wait for God to answer our prayers. Why? Because that's what faith looks like. It's how we demonstrate our trust that God is working all things together for our good.

Father in heaven, there are times I give up too easily. I lose hope or focus, and I quit asking You to help me. Strengthen me to be steadfast as I wait for You to answer me. Build my confidence to know You're working on my behalf. In the name of Jesus I pray. Amen.

WHEN WE DON'T KNOW HOW TO PRAY

So Jesus taught them this prayer: "Our heavenly Father, may the glory of your name be the center on which our life turns. May your Holy Spirit come upon us and cleanse us. Manifest your kingdom on earth. And give us our needed bread for the coming day. Forgive our sins as we ourselves release forgiveness to those who have wronged us. And rescue us every time we face tribulations."

LUKE 11:2–4 TPT

When the disciples were unsure about how to pray, Jesus laid it out for them. He gave them structure. He gave them cadence. He showed them the hierarchy, the order, of what to pray. His example revealed what topics to cover. And He gave them words to pray back to the Father. You know what? God will do the same thing for you. If you're not sure how to pray or what to pray, tell Him. Let the Lord know you're confused. Let Him know you aren't sure how to say what you're feeling. Then watch as He drops instructions into your heart. They may be loose or specific, but God will help you pray. It will boost your confidence and give you direction as you talk to your heavenly Father.

Father in heaven, sometimes prayer is confusing, and I feel silly trying to figure it out. Will You teach me how to pray? In the name of Jesus I pray. Amen.

GOD IS THE ONLY PERFECT PARENT

"If imperfect parents know how to lovingly take care of their children and give them what they need, how much more will the perfect heavenly Father give the Holy Spirit's fullness when his children ask him."

LUKE 11:13 TPT

Maybe you didn't grow up with the best parents. Maybe they weren't around much or didn't give you the love you deserved. Maybe they were abusive, and it deeply skewed the way you look at those in authority. And maybe because of the negative impression left by your mom and dad, you battle to see God as a loving Father. If you struggle to trust, tell Him. If you doubt God's goodness, tell Him. If you're afraid to believe, tell Him. If you're unable to forgive your earthly parents, tell Him. Ask the Lord to heal your wounds and transform your heart, because He is the only one who can. The only perfect parent is your Father in heaven. And when you pray for God to restore your broken and battered heart, He will fill you—His beloved child—with the healing of His powerful Spirit.

Father in heaven, so much healing needs to happen in my heart when it comes to my childhood experiences with my parents. It's a blessing to know my heavenly Father can love me with perfection. Help me take full advantage of a life with You leading the way. In the name of Jesus I pray. Amen.

GOD WILL ANSWER
YOUR PRAYER

While Jeremiah was still locked up in jail, a second Message from GOD was given to him: "This is GOD's Message, the God who made earth, made it livable and lasting, known everywhere as GOD: 'Call to me and I will answer you. I'll tell you marvelous and wondrous things that you could never figure out on your own.'"

JEREMIAH 33:1–3 MSG

This passage of scripture confirms that when you pray to the Lord, He will answer. Every time you ask for strength, it will be given. When you need wisdom or discernment to figure out your next step, God will open your eyes. If you need hope, He will hear your cry for it and deliver. Are you needing peace during a difficult season? God will fill your heart with it. Looking for motivation or endurance to stay present in a relationship? He will bless your request. The Lord knows there are things we cannot figure out ourselves. By design, we need our Creator's help to live and love well. And that is why He promises to listen for our voices and bless us with an answer every time we call out to Him.

Father in heaven, I know You can hear me talking to You right now. And I know You're already working on the perfect answer to meet my needs. Thank You for that! In the name of Jesus I pray. Amen.

EVEN JESUS PRAYED

*Then he walked a short distance away, and overcome
with grief, he threw himself facedown on the ground and
prayed, "My Father, if there is any way you can deliver me
from this suffering, please take it from me. Yet what I want
is not important, for I only desire to fulfill your plan for me."
Then an angel from heaven appeared to strengthen him.*

MATTHEW 26:39 TPT

Yes, even Jesus prayed. Today's passage reveals the depth of His grief and how He took it right to the Father. What a privilege to have this story in the Bible because it shows us His humanity. We get to see the Son of God draped in human skin. He stepped down from His throne in the heavens to experience what His creation experienced on the earth. So when you feel as if you're praying to a lofty God who can't relate, remember He understands because He lived it. We may never know the complexity of emotions Jesus was battling in this moment, but we do know He knew the weightiness of the cross coming His way. He needed strength to do what needed to be done. He understood His desires weren't what mattered the most but rather what His Father wanted. And just as we receive help and a blessing from prayer, Jesus did too, by way of an angel.

Father in heaven, thank You. In the name of Jesus I pray. Amen.

SUPPORTING OTHERS IN PRAYER

*Later, he came back to his three disciples and found them all
sound asleep. He awakened Peter and said to him, "Could
you not stay awake with me for even one hour? Keep alert
and pray that you'll be spared from this time of testing. Your
spirit is eager enough, but your humanity is weak."*

MATTHEW 26:40–41 TPT

You have the ability to bless people through your prayers and your
attention to their situation. It matters knowing others are standing
with us, because we recognize there are some struggles we cannot
navigate alone. Just as Jesus experienced, it can be a frustrating letdown when the ones you ask for support don't follow through. When
they fall asleep on the job and forget the battle you're engaged in, it's
hurtful. So decide that from today forward when someone asks you
to be a prayer partner as they walk through difficult circumstances,
you will honor their request. You will recognize their burden and bless
them. The truth is we all need community to come alongside us as we
navigate the tough seasons of life.

**Father in heaven, help me be the kind of friend who makes
a promise to support others in prayer and follows through.
Let me be trustworthy to cover them in prayer until the end.
And bless me with the same kind of friends. I understand
the importance of both. In the name of Jesus I pray. Amen.**

A BOLD CALL TO PRAYER

Pray always. Pray in the Spirit. Pray about everything in
every way you know how! And keeping all this in mind,
pray on behalf of God's people. Keep on praying feverishly,
and be on the lookout until evil has been stayed.
EPHESIANS 6:18 VOICE

This is a bold call to pray. Paul isn't mincing words or veiling the truth. He is direct in reminding us to pray feverishly all the time about everything in every way we know to pray. Why is he so insistent? Maybe it's because he knows that the struggles we will face in this life are not against flesh and blood. You may be able to see the Goliaths in front of you, but they are compelled by darkness. These forces stay hidden, tucked away and unseen, but they are wreaking havoc on your relationships. They are trying to destroy the children around you. They are actively working to mess you up. Don't let this scare you, friend! Instead, take Paul's command to stand firm in God's power through prayer, and watch as He blesses you. The Enemy's threat against us is real, but when we pray, we unleash the Lord's might.

Father in heaven, thank You for the reminder of how powerful my prayers are against the forces of evil. They may be plotting against me every day, but when I pray, Your blessings will abound. You will equip me for every battle. In the name of Jesus I pray. Amen.

PRAYING FOR THOSE IN GOVERNMENT

The first thing I want you to do is pray. Pray every way you know how, for everyone you know. Pray especially for rulers and their governments to rule well so we can be quietly about our business of living simply, in humble contemplation. This is the way our Savior God wants us to live.
1 TIMOTHY 2:1–3 MSG

When we look at the state of our nation and world, it doesn't take much to realize how badly we need to be praying. Regardless of what political party you belong to, which state you reside in, or how you feel about politics in general, the Bible is clear in its call to pray for our rulers and governments. That needs to be important to us. When we pray, it will be a step forward for our leaders to use their authority wisely. It will help them do their job with our best interests in mind. And the blessing will be that we can go simply and humbly about our lives. Just as it is for anyone, anywhere, there are ample opportunities for those in government to fall prey to temptation. Money and power are big lures, especially when a person feels invincible. So be a woman who prays for those in authority regularly. God will hear it and act.

Father in heaven, I may not be very political, but I understand the importance of praying for our leaders' integrity. Bless us all by their choices. In the name of Jesus I pray. Amen.

ASKING OTHERS TO PRAY FOR YOU

And please pray for me. Pray that truth will be with me before I even open my mouth. Ask the Spirit to guide me while I boldly defend the mystery that is the good news— for which I am an ambassador in chains—so pray that I can bravely pronounce the truth, as I should do.

EPHESIANS 6:19–20 VOICE

Paul never shied away from asking those around him to pray on his behalf. He even told them the words to share with the Lord. Paul got very detailed about what he needed from God, trusting people to specifically ask for it. Why? Because he understood the power and blessing it would bring forth. Let his example be what compels you to ask for prayer from family and friends too. As the Church, part of our burden and privilege is to storm the gates of heaven with petitions and prayers of thanksgiving both for ourselves and for those around us. It's the most powerful weapon we have in our spiritual-warfare arsenal. So don't shy away from sharing your requests. Let others know what your needs are. Tell them what to ask God to do for you. And feel the blessing that comes from a praying community of believers.

Father in heaven, hear the prayers of my warriors!
In the name of Jesus I pray. Amen.

EVERY WORD FROM MY MOUTH

Pray diligently. Stay alert, with your eyes wide open in gratitude. Don't forget to pray for us, that God will open doors for telling the mystery of Christ, even while I'm locked up in this jail. Pray that every time I open my mouth I'll be able to make Christ plain as day to them.

COLOSSIANS 4:2–4 MSG

What a prayer request by Paul! His hope was that his words would always point to the Lord. Even while in jail—a stressful and uncomfortable situation—he wanted to choose his words carefully. Isn't this also our hope? . . . When we are frustrated with the doctor's care of our aging parents, we can make sure our words are meaningful. When a coworker is mean for sport, we can think before we respond. Every maddening interaction with our loved ones can be met with a thoughtful response. Our job on planet Earth is for our words and actions to point others to God in heaven. We are the ones to share the gospel with the world. So ask the Lord to bless you with the wherewithal to live and love with intention. The expectation isn't that you are perfect, but that you are purposeful.

Father in heaven, let my life make a difference for the kingdom so I can bless You. I want my words to be a neon sign that points others to You. In the name of Jesus I pray. Amen.

THE LORD IS CLOSE

Yet when holy lovers of God cry out to him with all their hearts,
the Lord will hear them and come to rescue them from all their
troubles. The Lord is close to all whose hearts are crushed by
pain, and he is always ready to restore the repentant one.
PSALM 34:17–18 TPT

Knowing God is close to you in your heartache changes everything because it's in these moments we feel so alone. We are confused, unable to make sense of what we're experiencing. And so often it feels as if there's a pit in our stomachs, and nothing brings relief. We're left with a sick, hopeless feeling, and we are crushed under the weight of it. Yet when we are filled with faith, our prayers are heard by the Lord. What's more, He promises to come to the rescue. God is always ready to bring healing and confidence when we cry out. And while we may not know what God's rescue will look like, we can rest knowing it will come. Let prayer be your first response when the trouble comes. God will comfort you in your brokenness as He restores.

Father in heaven, thank You for being close to me always, but especially in my heartbreak. I am desperate for Your help in this mess. Your presence blesses me, and I am so thankful for Your unwavering love. In the name of Jesus I pray. Amen.

BEING GRACIOUS
IN YOUR SPEECH

Use your heads as you live and work among outsiders.
Don't miss a trick. Make the most of every opportunity.
Be gracious in your speech. The goal is to bring out the best in
others in a conversation, not put them down, not cut them out.
COLOSSIANS 4:5–6 MSG

We all need God to help us with our tongues. Sometimes words escape before we can tuck them away, and they get us into trouble. If we're not careful, we'll say what we feel in the moment, which isn't how we really feel. It's hard to be gracious when your child spills orange juice on your computer keyboard. It's hard to be gracious when your friend cancels plans that you rearranged your schedule for. Being kind with your words is difficult when someone cuts you off in traffic. So this call to be gracious with our speech takes God's help. Pray every day for the Lord to slow your speech so you can measure your words first. Ask Him to bless you with the desire to speak blessings and not curses over people. And choose not to put people down in conversation, but instead be intentional to bring out the best in them. Let God help you.

Father in heaven, I really need Your help to use my words for good and not evil. Bless me with gracious words no matter how I feel in that moment. In the name of Jesus I pray. Amen.

MAKING GOD FAMOUS

Lord! I'm bursting with joy over what you've done for me!
My lips are full of perpetual praise. I'm boasting of you and
all your works, so let all who are discouraged take heart.
Join me, everyone! Let's praise the Lord together. Let's
make him famous! Let's make his name glorious to all.
PSALM 34:1–3 TPT

Psalm 34:1–3 is a great call to brag on God to anyone who will listen. We are able to have so much joy because He has made us overcomers. He fixed the unfixable—more than once. God saved and healed and restored us from terrible places. And we are blessed by His favor because we are His beloved. So, friend, starting today, make God famous! Share what He has done in your life that is worthy of praising. Give glory to the Lord for the new job you worked hard to get. Boast about how He worked all the dates and deadlines together perfectly for your move across the country. Raise a hallelujah to God because the bank error was in your favor! Let your prayers of praise ring throughout the heavens and the earth, for God is good—all the time!

Father in heaven, You are so good to me! Keep my eyes trained on You so I don't miss a blessing. And then let me brag to others about Your goodness until I see You face-to-face. In the name of Jesus I pray. Amen.

THE POWER OF STORY

He told them a parable, urging them to keep
praying and never grow discouraged.
LUKE 18:1 VOICE

Jesus told countless parables during His public ministry as a way of communicating His message. Storytelling is a very engaging and effective method to get a point across because it's relatable. When you tell a story rather than spout off a ton of facts, to-dos, or rules, it allows listeners to personalize your words. We may not talk in parables much today, but we have our testimonies to share instead. Our stories are powerful ways to reveal God's power in our lives. Sometimes just hearing that someone else has made it through a difficult time is all we need to cling tighter to the Lord. So pray for the Lord to open doors for you to talk about His role in your life. Ask Him for opportunities to bless others through encouragement. And through your story, urge people to keep their eyes on God as they continue praying for hope and help.

Father in heaven, thank You for the example of how significant a story can be to those who are battling discouragement and hopelessness. You've done so much for me, so I'm asking for open doors to share that with others. Bless me with ample chances to boast in Your omnipotence and to help build their confidence of faith in You. In the name of Jesus I pray. Amen.

FREEDOM FROM FEAR

Listen to my testimony: I cried to God in my distress and he answered me. He freed me from all my fears! Gaze upon him, join your life with his, and joy will come. Your faces will glisten with glory. You'll never wear that shame-face again.

PSALM 34:4–5 TPT

A beautiful blessing that comes from prayer is finding freedom from our fears. This is a huge deal since many of us battle fear more than anything else. And maybe, if you look back in your family history, you'll see a long line of women who carried fear with them. So often, fear is passed down through the generations. But you have the opportunity to live differently. You may be the one who changes things for the next generation. And when you grab on to your faith and cry out to the Lord in your distress, scripture says He will answer you and free you from every fear that's knotting you up. Just because a fearful heart is how it's always been doesn't mean it's how it has to be. Go to God in prayer, and let Him bless you with confidence and courage.

Father in heaven, fear is a big deal in my life. Please hear my cry and remove my fear, giving me what I need to stand strong. Bless me with faith to trust in You no matter what. In the name of Jesus I pray. Amen.

WHEN YOU LOOK WITH INTENTION

"For I know the plans I have for you," says the Eternal, "plans for peace, not evil, to give you a future and hope—never forget that. At that time, you will call out for Me, and I will hear. You will pray, and I will listen. You will look for Me intently, and you will find Me."
JEREMIAH 29:11–13 VOICE

God wants us to look for Him with intention and pursue a relationship, investing time and our hearts in it. When we do, God will bless us with His presence. Too often, we put Him far down on the list. Our busy days come first, and spending time with God falls in priority. But it's important we remember that He has plans for us. He thought your life through, knowing the impact you'd bring the world. God never planned for evil to invade your life, but peace instead. And when trouble comes, you can cry out to Him through prayer any time of the day or night. What's more, He says that when you seek Him intently, you will know He is right there with you. When you put God first and foremost, you'll see blessings as God powerfully works in your circumstances.

Father in heaven, what a blessing to know You have plans for my life that are for good. Help me seek You with passion so I can walk them out. In the name of Jesus I pray. Amen.

HIS MIRACLE-DELIVERANCE

When I had nothing, desperate and defeated, I cried out to the Lord and he heard me, bringing his miracle-deliverance when I needed it most. The angel of Yahweh stooped down to listen as I prayed, encircling me, empowering me, and showing me how to escape. He will do this for everyone who fears God.

PSALM 34:6–7 TPT

Sometimes we are stuck in situations and can't see a way out. Everything seems hopeless, leaving us discouraged that things will never get better. Can you remember the last time you were in a desperate circumstance? What about a time when you were left feeling defeated? Are you there right now? Every time you land in that place, cry out to God in prayer. Lift your eyes to the heavens and tell the Lord what you need in that moment. Not only does He hear you, but the psalmist says God will send angels to encircle and empower you. They will open your eyes to solutions through His power. And in His deep love and care for you, He will bring deliverance. You will experience God's help and healing. So pray always and watch for the blessing!

Father in heaven, I am feeling desperate and defeated right now. You know the circumstances weighing heavy on my heart. Meet me in the mess, and deliver me through Your power. I am unable to untangle myself and am desperate for Your help. In the name of Jesus I pray. Amen.

PRAYER IS PIVOTAL

*And [if] My people (who are known by My name) humbly
pray, follow My commandments, and abandon any actions
or thoughts that might lead to further sinning, then I shall
hear their prayers from My house in heaven, I shall forgive
their sins, and I shall save their land from the disasters.*

2 CHRONICLES 7:14 VOICE

If you've ever doubted the power of prayer, let this verse restore your confidence. When we pray with humility—when we pray understanding that God is God and we are not—our requests will be heard. When we are intentional to live according to His will for our lives by turning away from the sin that tangles us, our choices change things. Every single one of us will face disasters in this life. From broken marriages to the loss of those we love to financial ruin, tragedy is a part of life. But in His infinite love, God made a way for us to be saved and healed. And prayer is pivotal. It's central to God moving on our behalf. It is key to hope and healing. Never underestimate what a Father will do for a child who asks in earnest. Talk to the Lord about what matters to your heart and be blessed.

**Father in heaven, I'm so grateful You made a way for us to
talk to You because prayer is a powerful way to unlock Your
goodness in our lives. In the name of Jesus I pray. Amen.**

PASSIONATELY PURSUE

Worship in awe and wonder, all you who've been made holy!
For all who fear him will feast with plenty. Even the strong
and the wealthy grow weak and hungry, but those who
passionately pursue the Lord will never lack any good thing.

PSALM 34:9–10 TPT

Imagine what it does for God's heart when you intentionally chase after Him. Think how it must delight the Lord when you make Him part of your day. Knowing that, choose to worship Him with a sense of reverence. Honor Him for being sovereign. And since every good thing comes from God, take a moment to show your appreciation every time something good happens. From finding an epic coupon to getting a good doctor's report, let God know you see Him at work in your life. Acknowledge the Lord in your strength and in your weakness, being confident He is always with you. Friend, your resolve to passionately pursue God will bless you in unimagined ways. The time you spend communing with Him will always encourage your heart. It will build your confidence and courage. And you will never lack any good thing.

Father in heaven, give me a heart that longs to pursue You every day. Help me love with more passion. And bless me in scarcity and abundance as I lean into You. I trust You to meet my spoken and unspoken needs. In the name of Jesus I pray. Amen.

IT WILL BE GRANTED

I tell you this: if you have faith and do not doubt, then you will be able to wither a fig tree with one glance. You will be able to tell mountains to throw themselves into the ocean, and they will obey. If you believe, whatever you ask for in prayer will be granted.
MATTHEW 21:21–22 VOICE

What do you need from God today? Do you have a sick child who isn't responding to treatment? Have you lost your job and been unable to find another? Are you battling loneliness as an empty nester, desperate for community? Have you been hurt by the Church and need reconciliation? Is your marriage heading in the direction of divorce, and you feel helpless to change it? Have you lost a parent, and are you concerned the grief will never lift? These are the times we should be driven to prayer for God's intervention. This is when we should be on our knees asking for the grace to walk it out. When we place our faith in God, believing He is who He says He is and will do what He says He'll do, we can know with certainty that He will help. When we pray according to His will, we can be assured that our requests will be granted. What a blessing!

Father in heaven, thank You for reminding me to ask for what I need. In the name of Jesus I pray. Amen.

MAKING "PEACE" YOUR LIFE MOTTO

Keep turning your back on every sin, and make "peace" your life motto. Practice being at peace with everyone. The Lord sees all we do; he watches over his friends day and night. His godly ones receive the answers they seek whenever they cry out to him.

PSALM 34:14–15 TPT

The only way we can make "peace" our life motto is to ask God for help. There are too many situations that bring stress and anxiety our way, and no matter how hard we try, we're not immune to them. There are too many legit reasons to feel angry, especially when we experience injustice. Worry robs us of peace because we recycle our troubling thoughts. And this call to live in harmony with others is often a tall order. Community can be so very tricky to navigate at times. So unless we are relying on God to still our spirits and give us the desire to live unoffended, our best efforts will fail. When you ask Him for the grace to let "peace" be your life motto, the Lord will bless you with what you've asked.

Father in heaven, my hope is to live with a heart focused on peace, but I cannot do this without You. I don't have the strength. Sometimes I don't even have the desire. Bless me with the ability to live and love well so my days here are pleasing to You. In the name of Jesus I pray. Amen.

GOD IS YOUR BODYGUARD

*Even when bad things happen to the good and godly ones,
the Lord will save them and not let them be defeated by
what they face. God will be your bodyguard to protect you
when trouble is near. Not one bone will be broken.*

PSALM 34:19–20 TPT

In those moments when you feel scared, remember God promises to protect you. Scripture says He will save you. The Lord will be your personal bodyguard, sheltering you in His shadow. Can you see it? The truth is bad things will happen even when we do all the right things. We won't escape tragedy or trauma or trials while on earth. Many of us will face unimaginable loss and grief. But the blessing comes through knowing this momentary heartbreak won't take us out. We may get knocked down, but we won't be defeated. We may get kicked around, but we won't crumble. Life may punch us in the gut, but we will stand tall again. That's because when trouble is present, we choose to lift our voices to the heavens and pray for God to comfort our anxious hearts. We ask Him to stand guard over us.

Father in heaven, thank You for being only one prayer away from helping me. I know I'm not promised a problem-free life, but I'm so grateful to know You won't let me face defeat. You'll always have Your hand on me. In the name of Jesus I pray. Amen.

PRAYING ON EVERY OCCASION

Therefore, I encourage the men to pray on every occasion with hands lifted to God in worship with clean hearts, free from frustration or strife.
1 TIMOTHY 2:8 TPT

God wants to hear from us on every occasion. No matter what is happening in our lives, it should be something we want to share with the Father. Praying with authenticity and unpacking all the hard things clogging our hearts will let us continue on free from any frustrations that may keep us tangled or stressed. So, if your husband walks out the door and your marriage is over, share your anxious heart with God. If your daughter receives a huge college scholarship that's a financial game changer, take a moment and lift your hands in prayerful worship. If the news from the vet's office isn't what you'd hoped to hear, go to Him for wisdom. There is nothing off-limits to pray about. Nothing is too big or too small. Nothing is trivial if it matters to you. So choose to be a woman who talks to the Lord about the details of her life, and feel blessed for it.

Father in heaven, it will take Your prompting to remind me You want to know what's going on in my life. I'm not used to praying on every occasion. Help me invite You into more of my life. I know it will bless me! In the name of Jesus I pray. Amen.

BE A BOLD WITNESS

If you're listening, here's My message: Keep loving your enemies no matter what they do. Keep doing good to those who hate you. Keep speaking blessings on those who curse you. Keep praying for those who mistreat you.
LUKE 6:27–28 VOICE

It is difficult to love others when we keep a scorecard. When we are more focused on keeping track of what others are doing (or not doing), it causes us to take our eyes off what's really important. We begin to justify our nasty and negative responses to their actions. Rather than protect their reputation from the gossip train, we are the ones who drive it. And as things deteriorate, we lose sight of what God expects from those who love Him. We turn our backs on His hope for His followers. We end up looking like everyone else in the world, showing no sign that we carry Jesus in our hearts. But our job is to point others to God. Ask Him to help you shine His goodness unabashedly. Be a bold witness for the Lord, and He will bless you with perspective and purpose so you can glorify His name with your life.

Father in heaven, I most certainly need Your help to love my enemies, do good to those who hate me, and speak with kindness when mistreated. I know with Your blessing through prayer, I can shine brightly for the kingdom. In the name of Jesus I pray. Amen.

THE GOLDEN RULE

If you don't want to be judged, don't judge. If you don't want to be condemned, don't condemn. If you want to be forgiven, forgive. Don't hold back—give freely, and you'll have plenty poured back into your lap—a good measure, pressed down, shaken together, brimming over. You'll receive in the same measure you give.
LUKE 6:37–38 VOICE

The Golden Rule says we should be intentional to treat others the way we want to be treated in return. If we want to be respected by those around us, we need to show respect to them. If we want to receive kindness, we need to live a kind and loving life toward others. We must have a gentle spirit, treating others with compassion if we expect it back. This is true in negative ways as well. When we're careless and reckless with people we love, we may experience the same from them. When we refuse to forgive an offense, it shouldn't surprise us when we're not forgiven either. Ask God for clarity to see the ways you're treating others. Ask Him to open your eyes to see each interaction with discernment. And then ask God to help you be a blessing to the world as you're blessed in return.

Father in heaven, help me check my actions and attitude toward others so I can be living and loving in ways that bless. In the name of Jesus I pray. Amen.

TO LIVE EXTRAORDINARY

If you want to be extraordinary—love your enemies! Do good without restraint! Lend with abandon! Don't expect anything in return! Then you'll receive the truly great reward—you will be children of the Most High—for God is kind to the ungrateful and those who are wicked. So imitate God and be truly compassionate, the way your Father is.

LUKE 6:35–36 VOICE

Imagine how extraordinary our world would be if we lived this way. What if we loved our enemies, treating them with extravagant care? What if we were willing to share what we had with those who needed it? And what if we expected nothing in return? What if, like God, we were kind to those who didn't deserve it? What if we chose to love the one who acted unloving? What if we were known for our compassion? Friend, let's agree that the only way we could live like this is if the Lord infused us with His goodness. And if He did, if He blessed us to live and love with such beautiful intention, it would change the world. But we don't need the whole world to act this way for us to. With God's help, through lots of prayer, we can bless the world for Him.

Father in heaven, would You bless me with the desire and ability to be extraordinary and give glory to You in the heavens? In the name of Jesus I pray. Amen.

ARE YOU CONFIDENT HE LISTENS?

My purpose in writing is simply this: that you who believe in God's Son will know beyond the shadow of a doubt that you have eternal life, the reality and not the illusion. And how bold and free we then become in his presence, freely asking according to his will, sure that he's listening. And if we're confident that he's listening, we know that what we've asked for is as good as ours.

1 JOHN 5:13–15 MSG

Do you believe that God listens when you speak to Him? Prayer can be confusing at times. Sometimes it seems our prayers leave our lips and get lost in space. They seem to drift off, unheard by the Father Himself. And when we look at our lives through the eyes of disappointment, we wonder if the Lord is even paying attention. We're sure He's disappointed as well and has gone off to work in greener pastures. Friend, ask the Lord to grow your confidence in knowing you're heard; ask Him to help you trust that your voice matters to the one who created you, because when we have assurance that He's listening and interested, we can know that what we've asked for, according to His will, will be done.

Father in heaven, thank You for the blessing of being heard by You. Please build in me the assurance that because You've heard me, You will act in my best interest. In the name of Jesus I pray. Amen.

THE MORE THE MERRIER

*"Take this most seriously: A yes on earth is yes in heaven;
a no on earth is no in heaven. What you say to one another
is eternal. I mean this. When two of you get together on
anything at all on earth and make a prayer of it, my Father
in heaven goes into action. And when two or three of you are
together because of me, you can be sure that I'll be there."*

MATTHEW 18:18–20 MSG

The truth is God made us for community. He never meant for us to navigate this life alone. So while one-on-one time in prayer is a powerful moment, God wants us to know that when we gather with others, it's power-packed. Scripture tells us that when we come together and pray, it sparks God into action. And the more the merrier. What a blessing that God sees value in relationship. Do you pray with others? Do you make time to gather together as a church or a small group or a family and lift things up to the Lord? Don't miss the weight that community prayer carries. Imagine how it blesses God to hear a collection of voices storming the gates of heaven!

**Father in heaven, I don't think I realized how important it is
to pray as a collective. Thank You for scripture that points
it out so clearly. Help me facilitate this in my own life and
my own communities. In the name of Jesus I pray. Amen.**

WHY WE KEEP HIS COMMANDS

And whatever we ask of him we receive, because we
keep his commands. And by our beautiful intentions
we continue to do what brings pleasure to him.

1 JOHN 3:22 TPT

According to today's verse, why do we receive whatever we ask of God? It's because we are diligent to keep His commands. This action and reaction go hand in hand. Just as parents are more likely to loosen curfew for their kids when they show a pattern of following rules, God too blesses those who follow His will and ways. Every time we say yes to the Lord, He is delighted. He recognizes our choice to set aside our self-focus and honor Him. Our intentionality to live by His commands doesn't go unnoticed. As a matter of fact, there is a beautiful benefit to activating our faith and obeying. Talk to the Lord about where this is difficult for you, and ask for His help to do what's right in His eyes. We need God's help to live well.

Father in heaven, I admit it's hard to choose Your way at times. There are moments when all I want is to act out in ways that make my flesh feel justified. But I want to please You more, and I need Your help to do that. Please bless me with the steadfast resolve to keep Your commands every day. I need Your help. In the name of Jesus I pray. Amen.

A HEART TO FORGIVE

Later Peter approached Jesus and said, "How many times do I have to forgive my fellow believer who keeps offending me? Seven times?" Jesus answered, "Not seven times, Peter, but seventy times seven times!"

MATTHEW 18:21–22 TPT

Most of the time, it's not rocket science to forgive the one who offends you. Accepting their apology doesn't require much from you; it's an easy yes. But then there are other situations and people that make forgiveness difficult. The last thing you want to do is extend grace, because the wrongdoing doesn't stop. They are repeat offenders of your heart, and you want them to pay for the hurt they've caused. Then you run into today's scripture, realizing you can't do this without God's help. Now, God isn't advocating that you be a doormat. He isn't asking you to let others treat you poorly. Abuse is never okay no matter how you slice it. But with His help, you can find it in yourself to forgive with healthy boundaries of protection in place. Ask God for a heart to forgive. Ask Him to show you how.

Father in heaven, without Your help, this is impossible. When I am offended, it's so hard for me to find the grace to forgive. I come out of the corner with claws bared. Bless me with a softened heart, and help me trust You as I forgive. In the name of Jesus I pray. Amen.

GETTING AWAY TO PRAY

*While it was still night, way before dawn, he got up and
went out to a secluded spot and prayed. Simon and
those with him went looking for him. They found
him and said, "Everybody's looking for you."*

MARK 1:35–37 MSG

Sometimes we just need to get away to pray. We need to find sacred space where it's just us and God—space where we can let it out without worrying that anyone else will pop in. Even if we close the door behind us, there are moments when others in the house feel too close for the conversation we need to have with the Lord. We may not need to steal away every time we pray, but sometimes our hearts require it. Be kind to yourself and honor what you need. Do you need to get up early to take a walk and talk to God? Do you need to go on a drive and pray? Does the shower work? The back porch? The next time you're stirred to find a sacred space to connect with your Father, do it. It's a setup for a blessing.

**Father in heaven, I get this! There are times I need to feel
miles away from anyone here so I can pour out my heart
to You in private. Help me be intentional to create that
space when I need it. In the name of Jesus I pray. Amen.**

HIS FIRSTHAND EXPERIENCE

*Now that we know what we have—Jesus, this great High
Priest with ready access to God—let's not let it slip through
our fingers. We don't have a priest who is out of touch with our
reality. He's been through weakness and testing, experienced
it all—all but the sin. So let's walk right up to him and get what
he is so ready to give. Take the mercy, accept the help.*

HEBREWS 4:14–16 MSG

What a blessing to realize everything we face in this life—every temptation or testing—was experienced by Jesus on earth. There is nothing we could talk to Him about that He doesn't have firsthand knowledge about. Some people say it's futile praying to the Lord because He's unable to relate to the challenges His creation may be up against, but that simply isn't fact. He is not out of touch with the reality we face as humans. To Him, it's not just book knowledge. Jesus lived it out on earth; He has real-life understanding. That means He recognizes our struggles and needs. He has compassion for the journey. And through prayer, we are the beneficiaries of His grace and wisdom as we take the next steps toward healing.

**Father in heaven, what a privilege to serve a God who gets it.
Thank You for knowing exactly what I am facing, because it grows
my confidence and faith in You! In the name of Jesus I pray. Amen.**

NAVIGATING THE WANT

You jealously want what others have so you begin to see yourself as better than others. You scheme with envy and harm others to selfishly obtain what you crave—that's why you quarrel and fight. And all the time you don't obtain what you want because you won't ask God for it! And if you ask, you won't receive it for you're asking with corrupt motives, seeking only to fulfill your own selfish desires.

JAMES 4:2–3 TPT

Oh what a powerful warning from James! We as humans are so predisposed to wanting what we want that we often compromise everything to get it. When we can't keep up with others, we become jealous. That leads to an inflated view of ourselves, which segues into hurting others as we jockey for position. We fight and argue to stay on top, selfishly focused on getting what we want. We play right into the Enemy's plan of division. But God offers another option, one that comes with His blessing. He invites us to ask Him for help, though we must first make certain our motives are upright. Ask yourself if what you're requesting is something of importance to God. Is it eternal focused? Or does it fulfill selfish desires? He is always ready to bless the faithful!

Father in heaven, help me keep my eyes focused on You when it comes to what my heart desires. I know You are my source for all good things. In the name of Jesus I pray. Amen.

THE TRUTH ABOUT ASKING

*Just ask and it will be given to you; seek after it and you
will find. Continue to knock and the door will be opened for
you. All who ask receive. Those who seek, find what they
seek. And he who knocks, will have the door opened.*
MATTHEW 7:7–8 VOICE

Be careful not to be deceived when scripture tells you that whatever you ask for you will receive. It's important we remember that God will bless our requests when we ask in accordance with His will. If you're asking for the ability to forgive someone who has deeply wronged you, you'll get it. When you ask for His help to love someone who is difficult and hateful, you'll be blessed with compassion to do so. The Lord calls us to forgive and love, so it aligns with His will. But if you ask for the money to go on a lavish vacation in the Bahamas, chances are it won't appear. Why? Because God doesn't want us to store up treasure on earth. His plan is for us to crave eternal things instead. Every time you go to God in prayer with a need that reflects your faith, He is ready to bless.

**Father in heaven, thank You for answering prayers. And thank
You for answering with great discernment, knowing what is best
for us in all circumstances. In the name of Jesus I pray. Amen.**

STAY CLOSE WITH GOD

*So then, surrender to God. Stand up to the devil and resist him
and he will flee in agony. Move your heart closer and closer to God,
and he will come even closer to you. But make sure you cleanse your
life, you sinners, and keep your heart pure and stop doubting.*

JAMES 4:7–8 TPT

Every time you move closer to God through prayer and time in His
Word, God moves closer to you. When you surrender control of your
life to Him, it closes the gap between the two of you. And that deep connection gives you courage and wherewithal to stand up to the Enemy's
schemes to destroy and discourage. It builds confidence to turn away
from traps set for you. Adding in repentance through prayer blesses
you as God cleanses your life, removing the blockage that keeps you
from following His will and ways. Remember, the only chance we have
to navigate this life with peace and power is to stay connected to God.
He will bless us with what we need to stand strong in our faith, ending
the free rein the Enemy has had in our lives.

**Father in heaven, move closer to me as I move closer to You.
Bless me with Your mighty presence as I walk out the ups and
downs life brings. Strengthen me to resist any evil that comes my
way. With You, I know I can. In the name of Jesus I pray. Amen.**

PRAYING ALL THE HARDER

*Don't burn out; keep yourselves fueled and aflame. Be alert
servants of the Master, cheerfully expectant. Don't quit
in hard times; pray all the harder. Help needy
Christians; be inventive in hospitality.*
ROMANS 12:11–13 MSG

What does it mean to "pray all the harder"? Sometimes prayer is confusing, and since it's not something we want to get wrong, we worry whether we're messing up. We wonder if our lack of understanding is why God isn't answering in the ways we want. And so we feel insecure and unsure doing what we think is right. The Word tells us to pray always and about everything. It says prayer is both praise and a weapon. We're told it's an important way to build our relationship with the Lord. So maybe praying harder means that every time our struggles come to mind, we pray. Every time we are stirred up by fear or stress, we pray right then and there. Maybe the idea is to start a conversation as we wake up and let it string through our entire day. Wouldn't that be an open door for blessings!

**Father in heaven, I would appreciate You telling me what
it means to pray harder. I know Your love for me isn't
performance based, but I want my life to please You. Bless
our daily conversations. I am so grateful to be able to talk
directly to You! In the name of Jesus I pray. Amen.**

ASKING FOR WISDOM

*Those people who are listening to Me, those people
who hear what I say and live according to My teachings—
you are like a wise man who built his house on a rock, on a firm
foundation. When storms hit, rain pounded down and waters
rose, levies broke and winds beat all the walls of that house.
But the house did not fall because it was built upon rock.*

MATTHEW 7:24–25 VOICE

Among the other requests you put before the Lord, let one of the most important be the ability to live with wisdom. We may be smart, but we don't have all the answers. We don't have all the solutions. And there will be plenty of times we simply don't know what to do next. That's why asking God to give us wisdom is so valuable. It's a blessing we have access to wisdom through asking. As we pray, we will begin to see the right path illuminate. We will have a deeper and sharper perspective on each situation. We'll be able to discern the right way from the wrong way with more precision. And our eyes and ears will be better trained to see God's direction and to hear His voice leading us toward the next right step.

**Father in heaven, please bless me with wisdom and
discernment to know the path You have for me. I want to do
what is right by You. In the name of Jesus I pray. Amen.**

BE A GOD-LOYAL WOMAN

*Prayerful answers come from God-loyal people; the wicked
are sewers of abuse. GOD keeps his distance from the wicked;
he closely attends to the prayers of God-loyal people.*

PROVERBS 15:28–29 MSG

Ask the Lord to help you become a God-loyal woman, trustworthy and steadfast. He is always looking throughout the earth for the faithful. God is looking for those who love Him enough to choose His ways over the temptations of the world. His hope is that we stay devoted day in and day out rather than allow our faith to be tossed around on the waves. Yes, the Lord is looking for committed believers. So each time you pray, ask for strength to be loyal. Ask for discernment so you'll keep company with those on the same journey of faith as you. And then watch as God richly blesses you with a holy resolve to stay the course. Watch as He provides encouragement through other like-minded followers. Watch Him answer your prayers in meaningful and mighty ways as you stay focused on Him. Your dedication will spark His delight.

**Father in heaven, don't be distant. Don't turn Your gaze
from me. Instead, let my devotion draw You closer. Hear my
prayers and know I love You! I'm committed to following Your
will and ways, so bless me with the determination I need to
walk it out every day. In the name of Jesus I pray. Amen.**

AN EVERYDAY EXPERIENCE

*My heart explodes with praise to you! Now and forever
my heart bows in worship to you, my King and my
God! Every day I will lift up my praise to your name
with praises that will last throughout eternity.*

PSALM 145:1–2 TPT

Prayer should be an everyday experience. Whether you set a specific time to connect with the Lord or you weave a conversation throughout the day, let it be a joyful expression of your love for Him. It's in these times you feel a deeper connection with your Creator. These moments allow you to breathe in His goodness. And just like any relationship you want to nurture and grow, it requires an investment of time. Let this sacred space be where you ask for help. Let it be where you unpack what is burdening your heart and causing anxiety. Let it be where you sit in silence as God brings peace and comfort to your weary soul. And let it be a powerful time of praise—a time when you express your gratitude for who God is in your life. Use it to recognize the ways He has blessed you.

**Father in heaven, help me make You a priority. I want prayer
to be an everyday experience that grows our relationship into
something beautiful. And first and foremost, I want it to be
filled with praises for Your kindness and generosity toward me.
What a blessing, indeed. In the name of Jesus I pray. Amen.**

THE REASON WE MUST CONFESS

*Rather, your sinful deeds have built a barrier between
you and your God. Your sins have made God turn his face
from you so that he does not hear your prayers.*

ISAIAH 59:2 TPT

This verse reveals why it's vital to confess our sins to God. It's why we must repent of our wrongdoing and change course. Because when we take responsibility for our iniquities and turn back toward the Lord, He lovingly turns His face back toward us with grace and forgiveness. Our relationship is restored! Friend, the truth is that our sinful choices create a barrier between us and God. They get in the way, making it impossible to be in a right relationship with Him. They block meaningful communication. When we choose to give in to a sinful life rather than try to live His way with passion and purpose, it deeply affects our relationship. And while Jesus' death has paid our sin debt, washed us clean, and secured eternity, choosing our flesh over His will causes a breakdown that must be fixed. How? Confess and be blessed! God is listening.

Father in heaven, I don't want anything to come between us. I confess my sin right now, and I'm asking You to help me confess future sin the moment it happens. My desire is for righteous living where Your blessings flow and my heart is full. I love You! In the name of Jesus I pray. Amen.

PASSING PRAISE DOWN THROUGH GENERATIONS

Lord, you are great and worthy of the highest praise!
For there is no end to the discovery of the greatness that
surrounds you. Generation after generation will declare
more of your greatness and declare more of your glory.

PSALM 145:3–4 TPT

Your praises are prayers pointing to God's goodness. Every time you whisper a thank-you under your breath, tell a friend how He showed up in your situation, or raise your hands in thanksgiving, those prayers of gratitude rise up to the heavens. Let this be an example you pass down from generation to generation. Let this be a beautiful family blessing. Make sure that the children in your life learn the power of praise! Point out every discovery of God's greatness to those around you. Tell those God stories around the dinner table. Recount them at family gatherings. It's vital we create an atmosphere of praise, making it a powerful tradition, because unless we are intentional to point out His goodness in our lives, it may go unnoticed. It's our privilege and burden to open the eyes of those we love to the reality of God's blessings.

Father in heaven, You're good! You're magnificent! Open my eyes to see it so I can open the eyes of those around me. Bring to light the ways You bless us. And help me create a tradition of recognition to be passed down through generations. In the name of Jesus I pray. Amen.

REMEMBERING GOD'S POSITION AS YOU PRAY

"For I will do whatever you ask me to do when you ask me in my name. And that is how the Son will show what the Father is really like and bring glory to him."

JOHN 14:13 TPT

Don't mistake this verse to mean that God is at your beck and call. He isn't a genie in a bottle, granting your heart's desire whenever and wherever. You don't control God. He isn't your personal assistant who makes happen the things you want. Friend, it's important to remember His position in relation to yours. There are none beside Him. None above Him. He's unmatched in every way. God is, has been, and always will be. He's all-knowing and all-powerful. The Lord is sovereign. So when you go to Him in prayer, asking for help, go with humility. Make sure your requests align with His will for you rather than focus on selfish hopes and desires. Ask in the name of Jesus, recognizing that He is where the power comes from; acknowledge the sacrifice He made. And when you do, blessings will abound, and your heart will be full.

Father in heaven, I see Your greatness. I recognize Your magnificence. And I am so refreshed by the ways You take care of me. Keep me humble as I pray, ultimately trusting Your will above mine. I'm blessed and grateful every day. In the name of Jesus I pray. Amen.

USE YOUR VOICE TO SHARE HIS GOODNESS

Your magnificent splendor and the miracles of your majesty are my constant meditation. Your awe-inspiring acts of power have everyone talking! I'm telling people everywhere about your excellent greatness!

PSALM 145:5–6 TPT

Let your voice be an instrument God uses to share His goodness and faithfulness with the world. Let it be what encourages people to trust Him when they're struggling. Let your words be the catalyst for someone to believe that He can heal a marriage, an ailment, a financial mess, a hurting child, or a broken heart. When you choose to open up about your life and the ways God has intersected with it in meaningful ways, you are sharing hope effectively with a hurting world. You're blessing others by talking about the ways the Lord has blessed you. Ask Him to open doors for you to unpack His goodness with those around you. Look for people who need to hear that miracles still happen through God's hand. And don't be shy to speak up and reveal the awesome acts of love you've seen from Him. Pray for those opportunities every day.

Father in heaven, use my story to encourage others. Bless me with opportunities to talk about Your majesty and goodness with a world that needs hope. And give me courage and confidence to speak with boldness as I share my testimony with those You place in my path. I'm ready and excited! In the name of Jesus I pray. Amen.

ASK FOR A VILLAGE

Back in the city, they went to the room where they were staying—
a second-floor room. This whole group devoted themselves to
constant prayer with one accord: Peter, John, James, Andrew,
Philip, Thomas, Bartholomew, Matthew, James (son of Alphaeus),
Simon (the Zealot), Judas (son of James), a number of women
including Mary (Jesus' mother), and some of Jesus' brothers.

ACTS 1:13–14 VOICE

This passage sets a precedent for the need for community prayer—men and women together lifting their requests to the Father is beautiful. There are some situations where it's more appropriate that we create our own sacred space and pray to God solo. There are other times when we gather a few close friends to come alongside us as reinforcements as we ask Him to help remedy a tough circumstance. But there are also moments when a collective prayer with a trusted community is exactly what's needed. Who are the people you would trust to stand with you as you lift your voices to God? Do you have a small group or a church family? Maybe you have a circle of friends who support each other through life. If you don't, ask the Lord to bless you with a village of like-minded and loving people for this adventure called life.

Father in heaven, please bless me with a community
of caring believers as we journey through this life
together. In the name of Jesus I pray. Amen.

THE FLOOD OF HIS LOVE AND GRACE

Our hearts bubble over as we celebrate the fame of your marvelous beauty, bringing bliss to our hearts. We shout with ecstatic joy over your breakthrough for us. You're kind and tenderhearted to those who don't deserve it and very patient with people who fail you. Your love is like a flooding river overflowing its banks with kindness.

PSALM 145:7–8 TPT

Can you picture a river overflowing its banks? Think of how the water bleeds across the land and covers areas usually parched. It saturates the dry ground and rejuvenates life that has lain dormant, softening even the hardest of soil. When we're struggling, that's the kind of breakthrough we're looking for. We need God's love to jump the well-worn path we've been treading for years and flow into untouched places. We need His blessing to spill over and bring forth something new and fresh. And even when we feel undeserving because we're in this thirsting place as a result of our bad choices, God is kind and tenderhearted, flooding us with His grace and love. Let Him be the one to rejuvenate your weary heart.

Father in heaven, what a great reminder that when I'm parched and scorched by life, You bring waters of healing and restoration. Help me find peace again. And bless me as I give You the fame for being a God who floods those He loves with unfailing kindness. In the name of Jesus I pray. Amen.

ASKING GOD FOR THE BIG AND SMALL

Whenever crowds came to Him, He had compassion for them because they were so deeply distraught, malaised, and heart-broken. They seemed to Him like lost sheep without a shepherd. Jesus understood what an awesome task was before Him, so He said to His disciples, "The harvest is plentiful but the workers are few. Ask the Lord of the harvest to send more workers into His harvest field."

MATTHEW 9:36–38 VOICE

Jesus knew they needed more people to help. In all His power, He could have sparked others to come forward. He could have stirred their spirits to join in the work. But maybe Jesus instead wanted to teach His disciples the power of prayer. Maybe He wanted to show them they could pray for things great and small. Maybe this request was part of their training, letting each see that their needs should be taken to the Father. Solutions weren't always up to them to figure out. Let this be a reminder for you too. There's nothing too weighty or too insignificant to discuss with God. Be it relief from a headache or help choosing a paint color or the healing of an illness, talk to Him about your needs because the Lord is interested! He is ready to bless.

Father in heaven, what a gift to know I can talk to You about everything. You're my confidant in all things! In the name of Jesus I pray. Amen.

GOD'S LOVE IS BLENDED IN

God, everyone sees your goodness, for your tender
love is blended into everything you do.

PSALM 145:9 TPT

Look for God's love blended into His work in your life. Honestly, it may not always look like love. Sometimes His intervention doesn't make sense initially. But consider that a failed relationship may be Him saving you from abuse. A diagnosis and the tests that follow may be what finds something of bigger concern. Your child being arrested might be exactly what's needed to change his current course of bad choices. Being fired unexpectedly could be what lights the flame for you to go after the career you really want. There are times God blends His unfailing love into circumstances that look worrisome and terrifying at first. Sometimes He must rip the proverbial Band-Aid off so the healing can begin. And many times the only way change will come about is if God makes it happen: We get stuck in a rut. We get comfortable, even in dysfunction. So He has to be the one to get the ball rolling. Ask the Lord to open your eyes to see the blended blessings, and then thank Him for always knowing exactly what we need in each moment.

Father in heaven, thank You for seeing the bigger blessing
and doing what needs to be done for it to come to pass.
I'm so grateful! In the name of Jesus I pray. Amen.

LIVE EXPECTANT FOR HIS RETURN

*"Be careful that you never allow your hearts to grow cold.
Be careful that you are not caught off guard, or your hearts will
be weighed down with carousing, drunkenness, and the worries of
this life, and that day will come upon you suddenly like a trap. Don't
let me come and find you drunk or living carelessly like everyone
else. For that day will come as a shocking surprise to all."*

LUKE 21:34–35 TPT

Jesus was warning His followers to stay awake and watch for His return. With all the unhealthy and immoral distractions the world offered, Jesus' cautioning was for good reason. He knew the temptation to give in to fleshly desires was real and easy to fall prey to. . *,just like today.* We are surrounded by carnal pleasures at every turn, and it takes bold determination to choose the path of faith instead. Friend, ask God to bless you with wisdom and discernment so you can make the right choices. Ask for strength to say no to sinful things. And prepare your heart for Jesus' return because it's coming. Today we're one day closer to seeing Him face-to-face. Let's make sure that when we do, He'll find us doing His work.

**Father in heaven, I don't dread the end. Instead,
I find myself excited to see You! Help me make good
choices so You'll be honored by the life I'm living at
Your return. In the name of Jesus I pray. Amen.**

PRAISING IS OUR PURPOSE

Everything you have made will praise you, fulfilling its purpose. And all your godly ones will be found bowing before you. They will tell the world of the lavish splendor of your kingdom and preach about your limitless power.

PSALM 145:10–11 TPT

Praising the Lord is part of our purpose. Showing Him our gratitude is part of living a faith-filled life. God is worthy of our adoration! So think about it: How do you praise the Lord? In what ways do you show thanks for all He's done in your life? Maybe you carve out time each day to spend in His presence and recount His goodness. Maybe you sing worship songs at the top of your lungs while driving to and from work. Maybe you journal about His faithfulness or create posts on social media that brag about Him. Maybe you share your testimony with those who will listen. Don't miss any opportunity to give the glory to God. Bless Him for blessing you. Tell the world. And as you crawl into bed at night, talk to Him about where you saw His goodness.

Father in heaven, my heart is full of gratitude for You. I see how You've blessed me. I know You've heard my prayers. And I don't want to miss any chance to share the beautiful ways You've ministered to my heart today. Open doors for me to tell the world of Your splendor and power. In the name of Jesus I pray. Amen.

HE OPENED YOUR EYES

"You claim to know nothing about him, but the fact is, he opened my eyes! It's well known that God isn't at the beck and call of sinners, but listens carefully to anyone who lives in reverence and does his will. That someone opened the eyes of a man born blind has never been heard of—ever. If this man didn't come from God, he wouldn't be able to do anything."

JOHN 9:30–33 MSG

Rather than boast about all your accomplishments and the good things you've done for others, boast in the fact that God has opened your eyes to see Him. He's revealed Himself through the Word so you can know and understand Him better. What a blessing to realize the Lord made a way for you to talk directly to Him through prayer anytime and anywhere. So choose today to live your life in such a way that it honors Him. Know what God expects from those who love Him, and walk it out daily. Keep His commands because they're the doorway to freedom. And keep your focus solely on God because He will help you navigate the mountaintop experiences as well as the deep, dark valleys. What a beautiful gift!

Father in heaven, thank You for choosing me as Your beloved. I'm blessed because You see value in me. Help me live in reverence as I keep Your ways because I see value in You! In the name of Jesus I pray. Amen.

WEAK AND FEEBLE NO MORE

You are the Lord who reigns over your never-ending kingdom
through all the ages of time and eternity! You are faithful to
fulfill every promise you've made. You manifest yourself as
kindness in all you do. Weak and feeble ones you will sustain.
Those bent over with burdens of shame you will lift up.

PSALM 145:13–14 TPT

What an amazing word picture to describe how we can feel. Sometimes life is overwhelming, and at the end of the day we're left weak and feeble. There are real-life, tough situations that leave us carrying a heavy burden of shame. Maybe we said our thoughts out loud by accident. Maybe we relied on ourselves too much. Maybe the wrong choice started a snowball rolling downhill that we could not stop. But in those circumstances that shake us and cause our backs to bend, it's the Lord who will lift us up. Our faith in Him changes everything. We will be blessed as He lifts our chins. He will restore our strength as we navigate painful moments together. And we'll stand tall as we see God's kindness and faithfulness revealed through His promises.

Father in heaven, Your works in my life are miraculous. I am so grateful for the ways You straighten my back and strengthen my frame for another day. Thank You for the way You bless me in each situation I face. In the name of Jesus I pray. Amen.

SIMPLY COME CLEAN

*If we claim that we're free of sin, we're only fooling
ourselves. A claim like that is errant nonsense. On the
other hand, if we admit our sins—simply come clean
about them—he won't let us down; he'll be true to himself.
He'll forgive our sins and purge us of all wrongdoing.*

1 JOHN 1:8–9 MSG

Many of us would rather hide our shortcomings than reveal them.
We don't like how it feels to point out what we've done wrong. . .so we
don't—sometimes not even to God. It's not that we think we're sin-
less; we just don't want to shine a light on failure. But unlike others
in our lives, the Lord isn't keeping score. There's no chart in heaven
that tallies up the number of bad choices we've made. And no matter
what, God's love for us will never diminish. You see, His desire for
us to come clean about our sins and take responsibility is because
doing that removes any barriers between us and God. That act of obedience triggers forgiveness and keeps communication unhindered.
So go ahead and confess to the Lord, and let His blessings of peace
and relief restore your anxious heart.

**Father in heaven, I am coming clean about my sin and
admitting the places I've fallen short of Your glory.
Thank You for being a safe place to be honest. Thank You
for forgiveness. In the name of Jesus I pray. Amen.**

GOD DELIGHTS IN CARING FOR YOU

You have captured our attention and the eyes of all look to
you. You give what they hunger for at just the right time.
When you open your generous hand, it's full of blessings,
satisfying the longings of every living thing.

PSALM 145:15–16 TPT

Let God be your source. Let Him be the one who meets the needs you have. As your Father, He delights in caring for His beloved. And because He's a jealous God, He doesn't want you looking anywhere else for the help He can provide. Ask the Lord to intervene and lead you out of the valley of darkness. Ask Him to supply the basics you're lacking—food, money, car, home. Ask God to bring a community of friends or a church family. Ask for healing from a medical diagnosis that has no good outcome. Friend, pray with fervor and expectation, trusting that He will satisfy every longing in His perfect way and in His perfect timing. Let Him capture your attention with His goodness. And watch as God opens His generous hand in response to your honest prayers.

Father in heaven, thank You for promising to meet my
needs according to Your perfect will. I know every good
thing comes from You, so thank You for blessing me so
richly. I'll always look to You as my source of satisfaction
and fulfillment. In the name of Jesus I pray. Amen.

DON'T TURN FROM GOD

The one who turns his ear from hearing God's instruction
will find that even his prayers are detestable to God.
PROVERBS 28:9 VOICE

Let this be a warning when we want to follow what our flesh wants. Let this be a verse that sounds the alarm bells in our minds when we're taking our eyes off God. The truth is we can't have it both ways. We can't live for ourselves and expect the Lord to bless us. We can't choose the path away from Him and think He'll join us there. It's when we repent of our careless choices and dangerous decisions that God comes close again. He is holy, and His desire is for us to walk in a right relationship with Him. It may be messy and imperfect. We may fail and falter on the regular. But God will see the condition of our hearts and know we are trying to be faithful. Be quick to turn back to the Lord and repent—He will be there with open arms, waiting for His beloved. And thank Him for embracing and blessing your return.

Father in heaven, help me cherish Your instruction and stay focused on the path that leads to You. Bless me with Your presence, and guide me in the right ways. I don't ever want to turn my ear or eye from You. In the name of Jesus I pray. Amen.

WHAT YOUR HEART REALLY LONGS FOR

*You draw near to those who call out to you, listening closely,
especially when their hearts are true. Every godly one receives
even more than what they ask for. For you hear what their hearts
really long for, and you bring them your saving strength.*

PSALM 145:18–19 TPT

God has a supernatural way of hearing what our hearts really long
for. The truth is sometimes we have no idea what we really want. We
struggle to grasp our real feelings, so we don't know what to pray for.
And the complexity of our emotions is confusing, leaving us unable
to untangle the mess inside. Friend, take a moment to appreciate
the blessing that comes from a Father who knows us better than
we know ourselves. He sees into the deepest places of our hearts and
has a perfect understanding of it all. When we pray, God listens closely
and responds abundantly. Embrace the matchless gift of being fully
known and fully seen by the one who can make a difference in your life.

**Father in heaven, it takes so much pressure off me to know
You fully understand what makes me tick. I don't have to
have it all together before I go to You in prayer. I don't have
to have clarity. You bless me in my messiness and meet
my every need. In the name of Jesus I pray. Amen.**

FRAGRANT AND ROBUST PRAYERS

O Eternal One, I call upon You. Come quickly! Listen to my voice as I call upon You! Consider my prayer as an offering of incense that rises before You; when I stand with my hands outstretched pleading toward the heavens, consider it as an evening offering.

PSALM 141:1–2 VOICE

The psalmist wanted his prayers to be something good for God. He wanted his words to be fragrant and robust rather than a burden. He wanted the Lord to receive them as an offering—a gift. He hoped his requests and thanksgiving were honoring so they would be noticed by God. And as his heartfelt words drifted up to the throne room, the psalmist's desire was for them to be well received. Chances are you feel the same way. Even without giving it much thought, when you pray, your sincere expectation is for God to be moved into action. Approach prayer with a wholehearted genuineness. Be honest and authentic as you talk to the Father. And be blessed simply because you are deeply loved by Him. God delights in who you are, and He stands ready to help His beloved.

Father in heaven, I want my prayers to put a smile on Your face. Even when I fumble and have trouble expressing myself, I want my words to tender Your heart. Bless me with Your delight as I open my heart and share it with You. In the name of Jesus I pray. Amen.

WHAT IS PRAISEWORTHY?

I will praise you, Lord! Let everyone everywhere join me in praising the beautiful Lord of holiness from now through eternity!

PSALM 145:21 TPT

Take inventory of last month, and jot down what God should get the glory for in your life. Did He provide a breakthrough in counseling? Did He boost your confidence to step out of your comfort zone? Did the truth come out? Was your reputation repaired? Did the loneliness dissipate? Did the apology come? Maybe the pain went away? Has the depression lifted and you're feeling hopeful again? Friend, ask God to help you be quick to recognize the blessings He brings forth. Don't let any of them pass by without reverence and celebration! Stand tall and be confident as you share His goodness with others. What a blessing to encourage others by boasting in His faithfulness. We all need reminders that God is still active and in the business of miracles. And even more, make time for prayer, giving God praise for the wonderful ways He shows His love.

Father in heaven, I will praise You for the beautiful ways You bless me. Thank You for always knowing just what I need and answering at the right time. I am committed to sharing Your goodness and faithfulness with a hurting world that needs encouragement. Open the doors for me to praise You publicly and with passion. In the name of Jesus I pray. Amen.

GUARD MY MOUTH

Guard my mouth, O Eternal One; control what I say. Keep a careful watch on every word I speak. Don't allow my deepest desires to steer me toward doing what is wrong or associating with wicked people or joining in their wicked works or tasting any of their pleasures.

PSALM 141:3–4 VOICE

Every single one of us should take this scripture passage seriously. We know the words we speak can bring life or death to those we love. They can encourage or they can cut down. Our lips have the power to bless or curse. And we get to choose. The problem is that, too often, we speak before we think. We let a statement fly out of our mouths in frustration without considering how it will affect those around us. Rather than take a breath before we share what's on our minds, we recklessly purge our thoughts and cause offense. But if we take this prayer seriously and start the day asking God to guard our mouths, He will bless us with the ability. Giving Him consent to control our tongues will help protect the ones we love. And we'll honor the Lord by following His command to love.

Father in heaven, help me bless others and honor You by watching the words that come out of my mouth. I want to bless and not curse. I want to encourage rather than dismantle. Give me self-control. In the name of Jesus I pray. Amen.

FULL ACCESS TO GOD

"For here is eternal truth: When that time comes you won't need to ask me for anything, but instead you will go directly to the Father and ask him for anything you desire and he will give it to you, because of your relationship with me."

JOHN 16:23 TPT

When Jesus gave up His life on the cross, it bridged that gap between you and God that sin created. His blood washed you clean in the eyes of the Father. And because He sees you through the lens of what Jesus did, you are holy. You have full access to God through prayer anytime and anywhere. You can talk to Him directly, unpacking what is weighing heavy on your heart. You can ask for what you need to walk out the season of life you're in—be it wisdom, forgiveness, peace, strength, perseverance, hope, or a million other things. God hears your prayers and responds in the right ways at the right times. The Lord delights in blessing the faithful. So take every need directly to God. Flood the heavens with thanksgiving. What an awesome God we serve!

Father in heaven, thank You for Jesus and what His death afforded a sinner like me. It's a magnificent honor to be able to approach Your throne with bold confidence, asking for help and guidance when I need them. In the name of Jesus I pray. Amen.

FIXING YOUR GAZE ON GOD

My gaze is fixed upon You, Eternal One, my Lord; in You I find safety and protection. Do not abandon me and leave me defenseless.

PSALM 141:8 VOICE

Every time you choose to fix your gaze on God rather than the craziness around you, you will be blessed. When you stay steadied on Him, the fears of the day melt away. This means you focus more on His promise to keep you safe than on what worries you. You trust that God will rescue you from the mess, not let you sink in it. Rather than allow the unknowns to overwhelm you, you take the next right step God reveals through prayer. You wait in expectation for the blessing of His presence to overwhelm you instead of giving in to the stress and strife of the situation. Fixing your gaze on the Lord requires His help, and it's an ability He will give you when you ask. Let Him be the one who protects you, knowing your prayers for His presence will keep you from being defenseless.

Father in heaven, bless me with the steadfastness to stay focused on You in the difficult moments. Give me courage to ask You for help when I need it. And keep me from taking control of my circumstances, because I know I can't fix things on my own. I need You, Lord. And I need You now. In the name of Jesus I pray. Amen.

PRAYING IN THE NAME OF JESUS

"Until now you've not been bold enough to ask the Father for a single thing in my name, but now you can ask, and keep on asking him! And you can be sure that you'll receive what you ask for, and your joy will have no limits!"

JOHN 16:24 TPT

When you pray, asking the Lord to help or bless you in any way, make sure to do so in the name of Jesus. Why? Because that's where our strength comes from. It's His authority that allows us to ask in the first place. And Jesus' name provides the weightiness we need to place our requests before the Father with hope and expectation. There is unmatched power in the name of Jesus Christ. So as each of the prayer prompts in this devotional ends with "In the name of Jesus," be reminded of His sacrificial gift of salvation. Praying in Jesus' name shows honor and reverence. It demonstrates your love for God. So close each prayer in His name, and encourage those around you to do the same.

Father in heaven, what a privilege to use Jesus' name in prayer. I do so with joy and gratitude for all You have done for me through Him. Let His name be always on my lips as I recognize the blessings that come because I choose to believe in Jesus. In His name I pray. Amen.

THE PROTECTION OF GOD

Protect me from the jaws of the trap my enemies have set for me and from the snares of those who work evil. May the wicked be caught in their own nets while I alone escape unharmed.
PSALM 141:9–10 VOICE

Let this be a prayer you pray often both for yourself and for those you love. The Word tells us that in this life we will have trouble. We will battle against evil forces manifesting in our earthly enemies to trip us up. We'll face heartache and grief because of others. Just like everyone else, we will walk out seasons of deep discouragement. We will suffer loss, rejection, and betrayal. So when we fail to ask God for protection, it leaves us wide open to attacks. Let the Lord bless you with His shelter as you seek it through prayer. Watch as you reap the benefits of His presence. And while the difficulties will come, God will help keep your head above water. Traps may be set, but you will be blessed and protected.

Father in heaven, please bless me with Your protection from the snares I am able to see and the ones I cannot. Don't allow the Enemy to overwhelm me with the negatives. I pray that I instead stand strong in faith and in Your strength, trusting Your presence to protect and save me. Bless me with an escape route every time. In the name of Jesus I pray. Amen.

GOD IS GOOD ALL THE TIME

Sing songs to the tune of his glory, set glory to the rhythms of his praise. Say of God, "We've never seen anything like him!" When your enemies see you in action, they slink off like scolded dogs. The whole earth falls to its knees—it worships you, sings to you, can't stop enjoying your name and fame.

PSALM 66:2–4 MSG

God is so good all the time. That means every good thing you experience or receive comes from Him. Maybe it was a restored marriage or a proposal. Maybe it was adoption papers or a plus sign on the pregnancy test. Maybe it was loan forgiveness or an unexpected invitation. As believers, it's important to have our eyes wide open so we can watch for God's blessings in our lives. We need to keep our eyes trained on Him, waiting with expectation for tangible reminders of His love. And when we see a demonstration of His compassion or restoration, let us fall to our knees and glorify His name. Let us be filled with awe and wonder at the ways God chooses to bless the faithful.

Father in heaven, my heart is full of gratitude for the ways You show love through blessings. I will acknowledge You through both private prayer and public praise, giving You the glory for every good thing in my life. Thank You for blessing me with abundance. In the name of Jesus I pray. Amen.

KEEPING WATCH OVER YOUR SOUL

*"Keep a constant watch over your soul, and pray for
the courage and grace to prevail over these things that
are destined to occur and that you will stand before the
presence of the Son of Man with a clear conscience."*

LUKE 21:36 TPT

Pray for the courage to conquer your desire for the world's offerings. No matter what, don't let them be a driving force in your life. Not anymore. Ask God for the grace to be victorious as you stand strong in your faith. When you begin to feel your sinful nature pulling you to revisit old habits and hang-ups, pray. Be honest with yourself about the struggles you're facing, and be honest with God too. When the burden feels too heavy and your resolve is weakening, ask Him to bless you with strength. This is how you watch over your soul. This is how you stand before the presence of Jesus with a clear conscience. Friend, you will be faced with temptation, and it will win at times. Be quick to repent and clear your conscience. Let God help.

**Father in heaven, help me keep constant watch over my soul.
Give me courage and grace to overcome the sinful ways of the
world. Let me stand blameless in Your presence, confident in my
faith and blessed by Your love. In the name of Jesus I pray. Amen.**

THE GOD WHO IS LOYAL

I called out to him with my mouth, my tongue shaped the
sounds of music. If I had been cozy with evil, the Lord would
never have listened. But he most surely did listen, he came
on the double when he heard my prayer. Blessed be God:
he didn't turn a deaf ear, he stayed with me, loyal in his love.

PSALM 66:17–20 MSG

There are countless words to describe God, but sometimes we struggle
to find the right way to express who He is to us. For many, God is healer
and restorer. He's the one who's mighty to save. He's the Prince of Peace
and King of kings. God is comforter. He is redeemer. He's our source
of all good things. God is the giver of strength and wisdom. But one of
the most beautiful words to describe Him is *loyal*. In His faithfulness,
God stays with us. He fulfills every promise He's made. He doesn't turn
a deaf ear to those who love Him and aim to live the life He's planned.
When you pray, be sure to call out the attributes that mean the most
to you. It may be different every day, based on your situation. But let
God know who He is to you. Tell Him why His presence blesses you.

Father in heaven, thank You for being loyal.
It's refreshing to know I can always count on You
to show up. In the name of Jesus I pray. Amen.

ASKING FOR WISDOM

*If you don't have all the wisdom needed for this journey, then all
you have to do is ask God for it; and God will grant all that you need.
He gives lavishly and never scolds you for asking. The key is that
your request be anchored by your single-minded commitment to God.
Those who depend only on their own judgment are like those lost
on the seas, carried away by any wave or picked up by any wind.*
JAMES 1:5–6 VOICE

Of all the things you pray for on the regular, asking the Lord to bless
you with wisdom should top your list. Always ask for His discernment
to cover your decisions. While we may be wise and smart beyond our
years, we all need the kind of knowledge only God can give. Sometimes
we don't ask because of our pride. Sometimes it's because we forget that
God is sovereign and all-knowing. But sometimes we don't ask because
we're afraid our asking will anger Him. Let today's scripture remind
you that a request for wisdom won't ever frustrate God. What's more,
your dependence on Him will bless you with wisdom in abundance.

**Father in heaven, what a blessing to know You give
lavishly. Help me be fully committed to You and not my
own judgment so I can benefit from Your wisdom in
every situation. On my own, I'm helpless. But with You,
I'm ready for anything. In the name of Jesus I pray. Amen.**

BE VOCAL IN YOUR PRAISES

Give thanks to the Eternal, and call out to Him. Teach the people His
deeds. Sing to Him! Sing praises to Him! Talk about all His wonders.
Brag about His holy name; let your heart rejoice in following the
Eternal. Always follow the Eternal, His strength and His face.
1 CHRONICLES 16:8–11 VOICE

It's so important we are vocal in our praises to the Lord because it
has a supernatural way of encouraging everyone. When we hear
spoken words, we learn. Many of us are audible learners, so listening
to accounts of God's greatness grows our faith, even if we're the ones
speaking. When we brag about Him to others, it encourages them
by offering hope in their situation. And it also glorifies and praises
God when we recognize and acknowledge His mighty hand in our
circumstances. Ask Him to give you opportunities to call attention to
His goodness in front of others. Ask for open doors to talk to people
about God's good deeds. Embrace every opportunity to sing His praises
and talk about His wonders. We are blessed in sharing and others are
blessed in hearing.

Father in heaven, let me be vocal in glorifying Your name
because You're worthy of all praise! Open my eyes to see Your
wonders and deeds, and open my mouth to share them with
others who need hope in You. In the name of Jesus I pray. Amen.

WHEN YOU CHOOSE TO BE PRESENT

Don't run from tests and hardships, brothers and sisters. As difficult as they are, you will ultimately find joy in them; if you embrace them, your faith will blossom under pressure and teach you true patience as you endure. And true patience brought on by endurance will equip you to complete the long journey and cross the finish line—mature, complete, and wanting nothing.

JAMES 1:2–4 VOICE

If you're struggling in marriage, stand strong and press into God. If a company merger means the loss of your job, don't waver as you trust. If you receive papers revealing an unexpected court date, be bold. If grief from your parent's medical diagnosis overwhelms you, cling to God. Friend, when you choose not to run away in fear, even when everything in you wants to, some amazing blessings will come to pass. Not only will it cause your faith to blossom, teaching you true patience, but it will also build your endurance muscle for hardship. It will mature your belief like nothing else. And it will enable you to cross the finish line with passion and purpose, knowing you stayed present with God through it all.

Father in heaven, help me embrace the hardships that come my way. I know You'll use them to benefit me and glorify You. Let me be present and awake as I press into You for strength and grow deeper in my faith. In the name of Jesus I pray. Amen.

WE CAN'T LOVE OUR ENEMY WITHOUT GOD

"Your ancestors have also been taught 'Love your neighbors and hate the one who hates you.' However, I say to you, love your enemy, bless the one who curses you, do something wonderful for the one who hates you, and respond to the very ones who persecute you by praying for them."

MATTHEW 5:43–44 TPT

We need God to bless us with the ability and willingness to make "Love your enemy" our motto. There are few things more difficult than showing love to someone who hates you. It takes so much bravery to pray for a person who's made it their life mission to make you miserable. Yet that's exactly what God is asking. He even goes a step further and tells us to do something wonderful—something beneficial—for the very one who hates us. Unless the Lord blesses us with His supernatural love and compassion for the wicked, we're in big trouble. Loving enemies is impossible without God's provision. We need a willing heart and big faith to walk this out, and the Lord will supply them if we go to Him in earnest prayer.

Father in heaven, I know what Your Word says about having a heart of compassion for our enemies. And I also know I am helpless in my own strength. Please give me what I need to be kind and generous to the ones who hate me. In the name of Jesus I pray. Amen.

HOW TO BE HAPPY IN TRIALS

*Happy is the person who can hold up under the trials of life.
At the right time, he'll know God's sweet approval and
will be crowned with life. As God has promised,
the crown awaits all who love Him.*

JAMES 1:12 VOICE

Remember a time you faced huge obstacles and God gave you the ability to overcome them? Remember how good it felt knowing your difficult circumstances didn't have power to take you down because you chose to trust the Lord for strength? Don't forget the power He gives to cope. Too often, we give up or give in rather than stand strong. We try to weather the storm in our human strength instead of relying on the Lord to bolster our confidence. And rather than feel a sense of accomplishment, we feel defeated. When you include God in the trials you're facing, asking for help to navigate through them, your joy won't be lost. Your steadfast faith will be met with the Lord's approval. And you'll be blessed for choosing to trust Him every step of the way, happy to be deeply loved by God.

Father in heaven, remind me not to handle the hardships of life on my own. It only leads to defeat and depression. Help me anchor my trust in You as You bless me with a sense of joy and happiness, regardless of my circumstances. In the name of Jesus I pray. Amen.

LOVING THE UNLOVABLE

"What reward do you deserve if you only love the loveable?
Don't even the tax collectors do that? How are you any different
from others if you limit your kindness only to your friends?
Don't even the ungodly do that? Since you are children of
a perfect Father in heaven, become perfect like him."

MATTHEW 5:46–48 TPT

Today's scripture makes us examine the state of our faith when it comes to love. It makes us revisit how we treat others and how much effort we put into living right with God. When you think about it, finding the ability to love people we deem unlovable is difficult at best. Maybe (if we were to be honest) we don't even try. We consider them a lost cause and move on. We instead focus on loving the ones who reciprocate. But God is challenging us to go beyond that. He's asking us to love the ones who are frustrating and annoying. We're His children, and when we ask for His help, He will bless us with the ability to dig deep for compassion. Through Him, we'll be able to find strength and grace to open our hearts and embrace the ones who criticize and discourage.

Father in heaven, this is hard to do because my heart has been broken. Strengthen me to do as You have commanded. I want my life to bless You! In the name of Jesus I pray. Amen.

THE DIFFERENCE BETWEEN TEMPTATION AND TESTING

No one who is tempted should ever be confused and say that God is testing him. The One who created us is free from evil and can't be tempted, so He doesn't tempt anyone.

JAMES 1:13 VOICE

There's a big difference between being tested and being tempted. It's important we realize that any temptation we face is courtesy of the Enemy. Because he hates us and wants us to live in defeat, he tries to lure us from living by faith. He's the one coaxing us off track as we're walking a path of righteousness with the Lord. He's the one pushing every button, trying to trip us up. The Enemy wants us trapped in bondage to sin. God, on the other hand, tests us. Why? Because that's how He grows our faith. It's for our benefit, not demise. Testing proves our faith authentic and allows us to experience freedom from our sinful nature. How can you know the difference between the two? Well, shame is a by-product when you give in to temptation, but a sense of encouragement comes from choosing God's help through a testing. The end goal of temptation is sin; the end goal of testing is faith. Ask God to bless you with discernment to know the difference.

Father in heaven, bless me with insight to know if I'm being tempted or tested. And give me what I need to stand strong regardless. In the name of Jesus I pray. Amen.

THE DIFFERENCE IN GOD'S ECONOMY

"How blessed you are when people insult and persecute you and speak all kinds of cruel lies about you because of your love for me! So leap for joy—since your heavenly reward is great. For you are being rejected the same way the prophets were before you."
MATTHEW 5:11–12 TPT

Have you noticed how God's economy is so different from the world's way of doing things? It's a new way of thinking that changes everything. As we read in today's scripture, our countenance should be one of joy rather than sadness when we're being insulted for our faith. When we're criticized or mocked because we love the Lord, it should put a smile on our faces instead of a frown. Where the world tells us to be offended, God offers us divine perspective. And we realize there is a blessing that comes from enduring the opposition—a heavenly reward stored up. What's more, we'll find ourselves in the persecution club with generations of believers. Ask God to give you a heavenly viewpoint to understand each situation so you can stay steady when the Enemy comes against you.

Father in heaven, I'm grateful Your ways are higher and greater than I can ever imagine. Thank You for an economy that reveals what's eternal. Give me the confidence to be unshaken in persecution, knowing the blessings will come when I see You face-to-face. In the name of Jesus I pray. Amen.

ALL GOOD THINGS COME FROM GOD

So, my very dear friends, don't get thrown off course. Every desirable and beneficial gift comes out of heaven. The gifts are rivers of light cascading down from the Father of Light. There is nothing deceitful in God, nothing two-faced, nothing fickle. He brought us to life using the true Word, showing us off as the crown of all his creatures.

JAMES 1:16–18 MSG

Let's never forget that everything good comes from God. Every single blessing we receive is a direct result of His love and care. Whatever is desirable, whatever is beneficial—those things are gifts from heaven. Sometimes we think it's because of our hard work, a stroke of luck, clean living, or something random that sparks His goodness in our lives. But it's important not only that we recognize His hand in it but also that we give God the glory for it. Today, talk to the Lord about the ways you've seen His compassion in your life. Acknowledge the blessings and thank Him.

Father in heaven, give me spiritual eyes to see all the ways You have intersected with my life. Let me recognize it when Your hand is at work in my situation. As I think back to how You've blessed me, I'm overwhelmed with a sense of gratitude. Thank You for caring about the details and giving me hope and healing in such beautiful and meaningful ways. In the name of Jesus I pray. Amen.

SHINING YOUR FAITH

*"And who would light a lamp and then hide it in an obscure place?
Instead, it's placed where everyone in the house can benefit from
its light. So don't hide your light! Let it shine brightly before others,
so that your commendable works will shine as light upon them,
and then they will give their praise to your Father in heaven."*

MATTHEW 5:15–16 TPT

Scripture confirms that we are to be the light of the world. This means our lives—what we say and what we do—should point others to God in heaven. No pressure, right? But take a deep breath, friend. There is no expectation from the Lord that we're to be perfect. The goal isn't and never has been to be flawless. As a matter of fact, nothing highlights our need for God better than failure. Our weaknesses are relatable. And it's often when we try to appear faultless that others walk away. How can we compete with perfection? Just be honest in your pursuit of God, letting people see your deep reliance on Him for everything. That's how you shine your faith.

**Father in heaven, what a privilege for my life to point to
You. I take that very seriously and am asking for Your
help to shine brightly. Let me be authentic in my walk
with You, and let that honesty spotlight Your goodness
in every way. In the name of Jesus I pray. Amen.**

LANDSCAPED BY GOD'S WORD

Post this at all the intersections, dear friends: Lead with your ears, follow up with your tongue, and let anger straggle along in the rear. God's righteousness doesn't grow from human anger. So throw all spoiled virtue and cancerous evil in the garbage. In simple humility, let our gardener, God, landscape you with the Word, making a salvation-garden of your life.

JAMES 1:19–21 MSG

No doubt about it, walking out today's passage of scripture requires intentional time in prayer and a big dose of God's help. We simply cannot make this happen on our own. Sure, we may have a good week of listening first and speaking second. We may have a season when anger stays in check. Our desire and ability to live in a right relationship with God may be on track for a while. But if we want to be a blessing to those around us and live the way the Lord intended consistently, we need to humble ourselves and allow Him to landscape our lives through His Word. We need to understand God's commands for living and loving well and allow those truths to flourish in our lives.

Father in heaven, help me be the kind of woman You created me to be. As You bless me with that ability, let me also be a blessing to others. Let my life choices affirm and encourage those around me. Even more, let them glorify You. In the name of Jesus I pray. Amen.

PRAYING BEFORE YOU ACT

*After leaving the synagogue, Jesus went into the high hills
to spend the whole night in prayer to God. At daybreak, he
called together all of his followers and selected twelve from
among them, and he appointed them to be his apostles.*
LUKE 6:12–13 TPT

While we don't know everything Jesus prayed and why it took all night,
we do know that He made a big decision afterward. Let this be a powerful reminder that when we pray with great intention, it sets us up
to make good choices. Any time we spend with the Lord sharpens our
eyes and ears to see and hear His will. It helps us cut through the noise
to find our next right step. And it grows our confidence to follow the
path God has set before us. You don't have to stay up all night talking
with Him, but it is wise to invest time in prayer until you feel a clear
leading. Ask the Lord to bless you with direction and wisdom so you
can have assurance as you move forward.

**Father in heaven, bless me with the patience to commit
to pray until answers come. Help me spend time in Your
presence, waiting for guidance and direction. I want to hear
from You before I take the next step so I don't wander from
Your perfect will. In the name of Jesus I pray. Amen.**

LET YOUR FAITH BE ACTIVE

*Anyone who sets himself up as "religious" by talking a good
game is self-deceived. This kind of religion is hot air and only
hot air. Real religion, the kind that passes muster before God the
Father, is this: Reach out to the homeless and loveless in their
plight, and guard against corruption from the godless world.*

JAMES 1:26–27 MSG

Faith is active, not passive. It manifests through the words you speak
and the way you live your life. It's revealed through your compassion
for others and your selfless acts when it matters most. And when you
activate it, it means you're choosing to guard your heart from the kind
of corruption that comes from the world. When your faith is active,
it means it's operational and will hold up under the weight of oppres-
sion. If instead you're all talk without substance, you will fold when
things heat up. Ask God to bless you with authentic faith—the kind
that proves your belief. Pray that He will help you trust Him when it's
hard and choose His way when it goes against the world's way. Let God
help you follow Him with intention every day.

**Father in heaven, I don't want to be a wimpy Christian. I
don't want to be a woman who just talks a good game. Please
bless me with real, true faith that can stand up through the
ups and downs of life. In the name of Jesus I pray. Amen.**

UNAFRAID TO HAVE BOLD FAITH

"How favored you become when you are hated, excommunicated, or slandered, or when your name is spoken of as evil because of your love for me, the Son of Man. I promise you that as you experience these things, you will celebrate and dance with overflowing joy, and the heavenly reward of your faith will be abundant, because you are being treated the same way as your forefathers the prophets."

LUKE 6:22–23 TPT

It's crazy to think that when we are bullied or chastised for being a Christian, we'll be rewarded in heaven. Every time we experience hate, we are adding up eternal gifts. When people criticize, the rewards add up. In those times when you are rejected or abandoned for your belief, remember the promise of recompense. Let the pledge of blessings help keep you steady in the faith. Let it be what builds your courage and confidence to be unashamed of the gospel. And when you feel overwhelmed by negative responses from others, take it to God. Ask Him to build your assurance of eternal rewards for standing up for what you believe.

Father in heaven, give me strength to speak out about You. Help me share my testimony without fear. Keep me from giving in or giving up when I'm met with criticism for my faith. And bless me as I boldly proclaim my unwavering trust in You! In the name of Jesus I pray. Amen.

THE BLESSING OF COMMUNITY

Every believer was faithfully devoted to following the teachings of the apostles. Their hearts were mutually linked to one another, sharing communion and coming together regularly for prayer.
ACTS 2:42 TPT

There is a beautiful blessing that comes from community, especially when it is filled with like-minded folks. It has the ability to create a powerful synergistic experience that's unmatched. When people come together for a common cause, good things can happen. There's encouragement and an energy that drives them forward. Being faithfully devoted produces a sense of belonging. And standing with hearts linked in unison for God sets the group up for abundant blessings through faith. Let this be the cry of your own heart. Pray for the Lord to bring community into your life. It may be a small group from church, a collective of people with the same hobby or interest, or a tight-knit neighborhood. It may be all women or include men too. Regardless, ask Him to bless you with others on the same journey of faith. Then watch as He brings people into your world who are excited to do life together.

Father in heaven, truth is, I'm lonely. I'm anxious to find a group where we're faithfully devoted to You and mutually linked to one another. Bless me with community. Open my heart to others so I can grow and thrive. Let me feel like I belong and am valued. In the name of Jesus I pray. Amen.

CONTINUAL CONVERSATION WITH GOD

*Every evening I will explain my need to him. Every morning I
will move my soul toward him. Every waking hour I will worship
only him, and he will hear and respond to my cry. Though many
wish to fight and the tide of battle turns against me, by your
power I will be safe and secure; peace will be my portion.*

PSALM 55:17–18 TPT

The psalmist realized the need to pray to God throughout the day. He
prayed every evening, every morning, and every waking hour. That's
a lot of prayer! The takeaway isn't that we should sit and talk to God
while ignoring the necessary details of the day. We must tend to the
home, take care of kids, complete tasks at our jobs, go to appointments,
and the like. But as we go about our day, we can keep an open line of
communication with the Lord. We don't have to be seated or kneeling.
We don't have to be alone. Friend, whether you're at the grocery store
or the gym or the lunchroom at work, you can talk to God. So carry
your conversation with Him into every moment of your day and be
blessed by His presence.

**Father in heaven, be part of my day. I'm going to
start my conversation with You when I awake and
say amen as I close my eyes. You're my constant
companion. In the name of Jesus I pray. Amen.**

WHEN WE NEED GOD THE MOST

*Open your ears, God, to my prayer; don't pretend you don't
hear me knocking. Come close and whisper your answer.
I really need you. I shudder at the mean voice, quail before
the evil eye, as they pile on the guilt, stockpile angry slander.*

PSALM 55:1–3 MSG

Chances are we've all felt the way the psalmist felt. We've all been
victims of someone who is mean-spirited and verbally inconsiderate.
Every single one of us has felt shaken by the presence of evil in our
circumstances. Many of us are very familiar with guilt and shame.
And experiencing the wrath of people and hearing their upsetting
lies being spread about us may even be a regular and relatable truth
in our lives. Rather than hide from God or take matters into his own
hands, the psalmist cried out to God. Even when it seemed He wasn't
listening, the pleas continued in earnest. Sometimes what we need the
very most is God. His presence is the only thing that will calm us. So
be quick to reach for Him when life feels too heavy and hurtful. God
will bless you with relief.

**Father in heaven, open Your ears and hear me. Come close
because I need You. My heart is overwhelmed and You're
the only one who can save me. Please bring relief and hope.
My trust is in You! In the name of Jesus I pray. Amen.**

HE IS OUR STRENGTH AND KNIGHT

I love you, GOD—you make me strong. GOD is bedrock under my feet, the castle in which I live, my rescuing knight. My God—the high crag where I run for dear life, hiding behind the boulders, safe in the granite hideout. I sing to GOD, the Praise-Lofty, and find myself safe and saved.

PSALM 18:1–3 MSG

Let us never forget it's God who makes us strong. He is why we can be confident in the battles we face. He's why we can feel brave to stand up for what's right. God is why we can be fearless to take the next step out of our comfort zone. When the battle is ours, He infuses us supernaturally, giving us muscle to power through, because in our own strength, we can only be strong for so long. But there are other times when God is our knight, rescuing us at just the right moment and finishing the fight on our behalf. We're to stay safe in His shadow as He does the heavy lifting. The next time the heat is on, ask God if He is going to make you strong for the battle or battle for you. Friend, you're blessed either way.

Father in heaven, You have all the answers. . .and they're perfect. I'm grateful You bring victory either way, be it with Your own hands or using Your strength through me. In the name of Jesus I pray. Amen.

PILE YOUR TROUBLES ON GOD

Pile your troubles on GOD's shoulders—he'll carry
your load, he'll help you out. He'll never
let good people topple into ruin.
PSALM 55:22 MSG

How much better we'd feel if we would just pile all our troubles on God's shoulders! Have you ever wondered why we try to carry it all ourselves? When you think about it, it's such a blessing to serve a God who will graciously carry the burden for us. He is a God who will bring help when we're feeling overwhelmed. It's a beautiful benefit that comes with a life of faith. Friend, what troubles do you need to off-load onto God today? Did you get some bad news? Maybe the bill was higher than you expected? Are you struggling in a relationship and at a loss as to the next step? Is someone you love battling a terminal illness? Maybe it's just been one of those years. Right now, ask the Lord to take this heavy weight off your shoulders. Thank Him for the promise and blessing of relief. And thank Him that He'll never let those who love Him sink under troubles.

Father in heaven, help me. I am so overcome with
what's going on in my life, and it's left me feeling
hopeless. I need the kind of liberation only You can
bring. I need to feel Your presence bringing peace to
my weary heart. In the name of Jesus I pray. Amen.

A PRIVATE AUDIENCE
WITH GOD

The hangman's noose was tight at my throat; devil waters rushed over me. Hell's ropes cinched me tight; death traps barred every exit. A hostile world! I call to God, I cry to God to help me. From his palace he hears my call; my cry brings me right into his presence—a private audience!

PSALM 18:4–6 MSG

With all that's going on in the world, it's hard to imagine that God has time to bring us into a private audience with Him. We may wonder why He would desire to single us out and give us one-on-one attention. But our heavenly Father is jealous for time with us. He delights in who He made us to be. So when we feel threatened, God's heart is to save us. He's the one who can gently untangle fear and insecurity. It's the Lord who will silence hostility and loosen the knots that strangle our joy and peace. Every time we cry out for His help, our voices are heard, and God brings us right into His presence. We're blessed because we are His, and the Lord never tires of caring for His children. Let prayer be an automatic response when you're overwhelmed by life.

Father in heaven, thank You for always making time for me. Thank You for making me feel special and important. I'm grateful for the blessing of Your presence in my life. In the name of Jesus I pray. Amen.

WHO ARE YOU GRATEFUL FOR?

*Our prayers for you are always spilling over
into thanksgivings. We can't quit thanking God
our Father and Jesus our Messiah for you!*

COLOSSIANS 1:3 MSG

When you're praying, do you thank God for the people He's put in your life? Do you list off by name the ones you're especially grateful for? If not, maybe it's time to start. Chances are you pray for the struggles they're facing. You probably ask God to guide them as they pursue answers. When they're feeling hopeless, you most certainly ask for a strengthening of faith. But do you express thanks for who they are in your life? Friend, count each person of importance as a rich blessing from the Lord. Daily, show appreciation for your husband if you're married. Thank Him for your parents. If you're a mom, let Him know how grateful you are for your children. Recognize the value of your coworkers, boss, pastor, group leader, or neighbors. Never quit thanking God for your community!

Father in heaven, I can see how You've strategically surrounded me with amazing people. Thank You for knowing the right ones to put in my life. I confess there have been times I've taken them for granted and treated them unkindly. I'm so sorry. Help me remember how blessed I am to be loved by them, and help me love them in return. In the name of Jesus I pray. Amen.

OCEAN OF HATE
AND ENEMY CHAOS

But me he caught—reached all the way from sky to sea;
he pulled me out of that ocean of hate, that enemy chaos,
the void in which I was drowning. They hit me when I was
down, but GOD stuck by me. He stood me up on a wide-
open field; I stood there saved—surprised to be loved!

PSALM 18:16–19 MSG

When you're struggling with mean-spirited criticism, pray for God to intervene. When you're feeling judged by those who should love and cherish you instead, share the depth of your heartache with Him. In those times when friends betray your trust, cry out to the Lord. And then wait with expectation for Him to reach down from heaven and pull you from the ocean of hate and enemy chaos. God is mighty to save, and you can count on Him to bring liberation to the weariest of souls. Chances are He's already blessed you by pulling you from the pit countless times before. And chances are you stood there in awe each time, surprised that God showed up once again.

Father in heaven, thank You for being mighty to save.
Thank You for knowing just what I need right when I need
it. I'm blessed by Your relentless love and willingness to
rescue me when I'm drowning. Thank You for the constant
compassion You show me. In the name of Jesus I pray. Amen.

DEAD-END ALLEYS AND DARK DUNGEONS

God rescued us from dead-end alleys and dark dungeons.
He's set us up in the kingdom of the Son he loves so much,
the Son who got us out of the pit we were in, got rid
of the sins we were doomed to keep repeating.
COLOSSIANS 1:13–14 MSG

One of the most valuable and kind blessings we receive from God is being rescued from dead-end alleys and dark dungeons. This is not literal but symbolic of where we often find ourselves in life. It may be a battle with an addiction. It may be a dangerous path of temptation we're walking down. It may be a bout of depression or hopelessness. Maybe it's a secret life we're living that no one else knows about. It might even be a mess that our current choices will cause if we don't make a change. There is no one who can pull us from the pit better than the Lord. So no matter where you are right now or where you're headed, grab on to the Savior. He's your greatest hope and worthy of your trust. And when you cry out for help, God will be there for you.

Father in heaven, help me. I'm trapped in the pit of despair and need help. Open my eyes to truth and bring relief. Save me from this mess. And let me experience the power of Your presence in my situation. In the name of Jesus I pray. Amen.

GOD CAN PIECE YOUR LIFE BACK TOGETHER

GOD made my life complete when I placed all the pieces before him. When I got my act together, he gave me a fresh start. Now I'm alert to GOD's ways; I don't take God for granted. Every day I review the ways he works; I try not to miss a trick. I feel put back together, and I'm watching my step. GOD rewrote the text of my life when I opened the book of my heart to his eyes.

PSALM 18:20–24 MSG

When you pray and ask God to work in your life, to put you back together, He will. Sometimes it takes awhile to get our act together and give every broken piece to the Lord for healing. Try as we might, we're simply unable to restore ourselves. We don't have that kind of power. There is no facial, weight-loss program, counseling session, or yoga class that can restore our souls. The bottom line is that we need Him. Desperately. Ask God to bless you with the spiritual eyes to see His work. Ask for the memory to recall His goodness in the past. And be in awe of the ways He pours into your life here and now.

Father in heaven, help me be alert to Your ways and never take them for granted. I know I'm deeply loved and cared for. I see it manifest in beautiful ways. In the name of Jesus I pray. Amen.

APPROACHING GOD WITH REVERENCE

When Jesus was on the earth, a man of flesh and blood,
He offered up prayers and pleas, groans and tears to the One
who could save Him from death. He was heard because He
approached God with reverence. Although He was a Son,
Jesus learned obedience through the things He suffered.
HEBREWS 5:7–8 VOICE

Don't miss today's revelation, because it may be the key to unlocking your prayers that seem to bounce off the ceiling. Have you been asking God to heal a marriage? Have you asked for wisdom in a big decision? Maybe you've been praying for financial relief or physical healing? If it feels like God isn't hearing you, maybe you need to look at how you're approaching the throne. Are you being flippant? Are you just repeating the same old words without the emotion behind them? Are you being demanding? When Jesus approached His Father, He did so with reverence. He came with respect and devotion. Scripture says that because of this position, He was heard. If you're struggling with your prayer life, take inventory of your heart. See if anything in you needs to change. Then get ready for the blessing.

Father in heaven, I don't ever want to be disrespectful in prayer, so please forgive me for the times I've been irreverent. Help me remember my position in relation to Yours. And bless me as Your will in my life is done. In the name of Jesus I pray. Amen.

ASKING GOD TO FLOODLIGHT YOUR LIFE

*Suddenly, GOD, you floodlight my life; I'm blazing with glory,
God's glory! I smash the bands of marauders, I vault the
highest fences. What a God! His road stretches straight
and smooth. Every GOD-direction is road-tested.
Everyone who runs toward him makes it.*

PSALM 18:28–30 MSG

When life feels gloomy, look to God to floodlight your way because His light brings clarity and understanding. God has a supernatural way of brightening the darkness that brings fear and insecurity, helping us find our footing so we can stand strong. His light reveals what is true and dismisses any confusion that clouds our discernment. And it invigorates our spirits so we can confidently trust His leading. With Him, we're victorious! Let it be a blessing to know the power of God in your life. His ways are without fault, and His Word is authentic. You can trust Him to keep you protected and on the right path. So no matter what, choose to follow God. And at every crossroads you come to, ask for direction.

Father in heaven, sometimes the right path and the wrong path look the same. I get confused and struggle to know what's best. But I am blessed by Your perfect and powerful light that reveals the path You have chosen for me. Open my eyes to see it and walk it. I trust You! In the name of Jesus I pray. Amen.

YOU ARE CHOSEN

*I don't call you servants any longer; servants don't know what
the master is doing, but I have told you everything the Father
has said to Me. I call you friends. You did not choose Me.
I chose you, and I orchestrated all of this so that you would
be sent out and bear great and perpetual fruit. As you do this,
anything you ask the Father in My name will be done.*
JOHN 15:15–16 VOICE

Friend, you are chosen. It may be hard to grasp the truth that the one
who created the heavens and the earth and everything in them knows
you by name. Since God thought you up, it means He has full knowledge of who you are. He knows the complexity of your emotions. He
knows what keeps you up at night and the little things that bring joy.
He knows your tendency to be annoying to those around you as well as
all the ways you bless others. And when God made you, He also placed
in you a great calling to bear fruit in His name. So learn to embrace
who you're made to be. Thank Him for blessing you with being known
and chosen. God is so good.

**Father in heaven, it's humbling to think You have a divine
plan for my life. What a blessing that You would even want
someone like me, knowing my flaws and imperfections.
My heart is full! In the name of Jesus I pray. Amen.**

HIS WRAPAROUND PRESENCE

You empower me for victory with your wraparound presence.
Your power within makes me strong to subdue. By stooping
down in gentleness, you made me great! You've set me free,
and now I'm standing complete, ready to fight some more!

PSALM 18:35–36 TPT

God promises to empower us for the battle. He makes us great through His gentleness and kindness. The Lord untangles us and sets us free from anything that keeps us paralyzed and unable to take our rightful place on the battlefield. And God is the only one who can make us complete, lacking for nothing as we navigate the circumstances we face. Be intentional to count those as blessings! Don't take God for granted. Kneel in reverence and honor for who He is in your life. Be humbled by His attention to detail in each situation. And embrace the confidence boost that comes from His wraparound presence. There is no one who can set you up for success like God, so praise Him for making sure you have all you need to move forward in faith and conquer.

Father in heaven, I trust You to equip me for victory. You have a perfect track record in my life, and I've seen Your hand move mightily more times than I can count. You're a God of blessing and abundance, and I am grateful You chose me to be Yours. In the name of Jesus I pray. Amen.

THE NEED FOR
GOD'S PERSPECTIVE

*If you find that the world despises you, remember that before
it despised you, it first despised Me. If you were a product
of the world order, then it would love you. But you are
not a product of the world because I have taken you out
of it, and it despises you for that very reason.*

JOHN 15:18–19 VOICE

It's difficult to be okay with not being liked. We may talk a big talk
about being fine with it, but it hurts. It feels unjustified. And it leaves
a pit in our stomachs. Let God refocus your perspective so you can find
peace in this chaotic world of haters. The reality is, when we choose a
life of faith and walk it out with integrity, it places a big ole target on
our backs. Some will dislike us simply because we love the Lord. Some
will despise us for our moral compass and character. And others will
feel judged, certain we think we're better than they are. Be blessed
knowing you're not a part of this world system. You're choosing to live
right with God instead. Pray for courage. Pray for confidence. Pray
for His perspective.

**Father in heaven, help me recognize that hatred from the world
is often an indicator I'm standing strong in my faith. Bring peace
to my heart as I meditate on Your truth and find strength to
continue choosing Your ways. In the name of Jesus I pray. Amen.**

SO THE NATIONS WILL HEAR

*He rescues me from my enemies; he lifts me up high and keeps
me out of reach, far from the grasp of my violent foe. So I
thank you, Yahweh, with my praises! I will sing my song to
the highest God, so all among the nations will hear me.*

PSALM 18:48–49 TPT

The psalmist said he sings so all among the nations will hear. Take a minute to think about that powerful statement. Of course we know it's not literal. He wasn't walking around with a megaphone. There weren't radios to broadcast far and wide. So he could have meant that praises to God for His goodness were always on his lips. Every interaction with others was an opportunity he used to share his testimony. He told so many that it flooded the area with stories of God's protection and compassion. People learned of His promise to save and restore. And word spread like fire. Ask the Lord to amplify your voice to your community. Pray for the confidence to unabashedly boast in the ways He's shown up in your circumstances. Always be ready to tell others about the blessings you've received because of His great love.

**Father in heaven, I want to encourage others through my testimony.
I want them to understand they can experience the depth of Your
love and abundance of blessings too. Open the right doors at the
right time, and I will testify. In the name of Jesus I pray. Amen.**

THE BLESSING OF THE HOLY SPIRIT

I will send a great Helper to you from the Father,
one known as the Spirit of truth. He comes from the
Father and will point to the truth as it concerns Me.
JOHN 15:26 VOICE

When you say yes to Jesus being your personal Savior, God deposits His Holy Spirit in you. He is the one who helps you determine right from wrong. He is often that gut feeling that gnaws at you to choose one way or another. The Lord's Spirit brings truth, opening your eyes so you can make choices that glorify God. And He is vital to living a righteous life. Take a moment to thank God for the blessing of the Holy Spirit. Thank Him for the power He infuses into you, which helps guide you to handle tough and challenging circumstances. Tell God how you hear His Spirit best, how you recognize Him moving your heart to stand strong. One of the most beautiful benefits we receive as His followers is the constant companionship and direction the Holy Spirit provides. Don't ever take His presence for granted. It's an unmatched blessing in the life of every believer.

Father in heaven, hear my praises of gratitude rise into the heavens. Your Holy Spirit is deeply valued in my everyday life, and I'm beyond blessed to have 24-7 access to hearing Your voice of discernment in my own spirit. In the name of Jesus I pray. Amen.

WHAT CAN WE NOT PRAY ABOUT?

Are you hurting? Pray. Do you feel great? Sing. Are you sick? Call the church leaders together to pray and anoint you with oil in the name of the Master. Believing-prayer will heal you, and Jesus will put you on your feet. And if you've sinned, you'll be forgiven—healed inside and out.

JAMES 5:13–15 MSG

What can we not pray about? When we dig into God's Word, we realize He wants us to pray in every way about all things. Nothing is too big. Nothing is too small. Nothing too trivial. What a huge blessing to realize that means we can talk to Him all day! It can be a string of prayers from sunup to sundown—an ongoing conversation that threads throughout the day. Maybe your prayers are praises that you literally sing, recognizing God's big move in your circumstances; you make up a tune, add in words, and lift your voice to the heavens. Maybe you need Him to guide you through a tough workday ahead, so you talk strategy with Him. Maybe you're battling fear and insecurity and talking to Him calms your anxious heart. From healing to help to forgiveness to direction, prayer will bless you in meaningful ways.

Father in heaven, what a blessing to know You are interested in every part of my life. There is literally nothing I cannot pray about. Amazing. In the name of Jesus I pray. Amen.

GOD'S HEART FOR YOU IS GOOD

*Listen, Yahweh, to my passionate prayer! Can't you hear my
groaning? Don't you hear how I'm crying out to you? My King
and my God, consider my every word, for I am calling out to you.*
PSALM 5:1–2 TPT

If you ever feel that God isn't listening to your prayers, think again.
When it seems you're talking into space and no one hears your pleas
for help, it's vital to remember that God's Word says He is always
thinking of you. The truth is everyone feels this way from time to
time. And especially when we're overwhelmed and feeling desperate,
our abandonment issues get triggered and we feel alone. This is when
we dig in and hold tight to faith that tells us we are loved and valued.
It's when we cling to the knowledge that God's heart for us is always
good. And it's in these moments we should ask God to exchange our
unbelief for His unchangeable adoration. Think back to a time the Lord
answered your prayer. Maybe you received peace, an opened door, an
apology, a dose of courage, or an unexpected blessing. Remembering
this, coupled with prayer, will calm your anxious heart and bring an
unmatched sense of expectation.

**Father in heaven, if there is anything blocking my prayers,
please let me know. Until then, I am choosing to believe You will
hear and respond every time. In the name of Jesus I pray. Amen.**

THE POWER OF YOUR WORDS

*"Take this most seriously: A yes on earth is yes
in heaven; a no on earth is no in heaven.
What you say to one another is eternal."*
MATTHEW 18:18 MSG

What a great reminder that our words matter. They mean something both here and in heaven. It's crucial we remember the power they hold not only in our lives but also in the lives of others. We can either bless others with our words or use them to curse. They can be a powerful way to encourage, or they can deflate someone. What we say can bring hope or dash it. It can usher in peace and confidence or crush it. So be thoughtful, but more importantly, ask God to tame your tongue. When you ask, He will give you wisdom and discernment so you are careful. He will help you be quick to listen and slow to speak so your words are measured. The world is hard enough as it is. Life kicks us in the teeth enough on its own. Let's not be women who add to the pain of others, but instead let's be women who use words to point to God in heaven. Let the Lord bless what you say so it's helpful and encouraging to those who need it the most. (And sometimes that includes yourself.)

**Father in heaven, let my words bring forth life.
In the name of Jesus I pray. Amen.**

AT EACH AND EVERY SUNRISE

At each and every sunrise you will hear my voice as I prepare my
sacrifice of prayer to you. Every morning I lay out the pieces of
my life on the altar and wait for your fire to fall upon my heart.

PSALM 5:3 TPT

Starting your day with prayer sets you up for a peace-filled day. It allows you to get your priorities in order so they're not jockeying for position. It offers you a chance to connect with your Father and set your heart right. It's an opportunity to share your needs with the one who can bless you with help. And it is a time to lay everything out before the Lord so your burden is light. Prayer is a blessing to the believer because it brings us closer to our Creator. We must guard against prayer slipping down the to-do list. Sometimes we jolt into action when the alarm goes off, and at the end of the day we lay our heads on the pillow without uttering a word to the Lord. Prayer gets lost in the mix. So unless we make time to converse with God, chances are we won't. Let God hear your voice at each and every sunrise.

Father in heaven, help me establish a routine of starting
my day with prayer. It's a blessing I don't want to
miss out on. In the name of Jesus I pray. Amen.

STAND FIRM IN GOD'S LOVE

You, however, should stand firm in the love of God,
constructing a life within the holy faith, praying the
Spirit's prayer, as you wait eagerly for the mercy of our
Lord Jesus the Anointed, which leads to eternal life.
JUDE 20–21 VOICE

Friend, you are so deeply loved by God. Scripture tells us to stand firm in that powerful and beautiful truth, never doubting the Father sees our significance. Be alert to the outside influences trying to dilute that truth, and don't let anyone talk you out of believing it. Whenever—and for whatever reason—you begin to doubt, pray. Tell God how you're feeling. Let Him know why you're struggling to believe a perfect God could love an imperfect person. Share how past hurts influence your unbelief. And then ask Him to reveal His love in tangible and recognizable ways that will connect with your heart. Being honest about your worries and fears deepens your relationship with God. When you surrender your control and pride and cry out to Him for help, your prayers will be answered.

Father in heaven, I confess there are times I worry You don't love me. It's hard to stand firm when I feel so unworthy. Bless me with the secure knowledge that there is nothing I can do to make You love me any more or any less than You do right now. Strengthen my belief. In the name of Jesus I pray. Amen.

SMOOTHING OUT
THE ROAD AHEAD

*Yahweh, lead me in the pathways of your pleasure just
like you promised me you would, or else my enemies
will conquer me. Smooth out your road in front of me,
straight and level, so that I will know where to walk.*

PSALM 5:8 TPT

What a relief to know God will smooth out the road in front of you. The reality is we sometimes find ourselves on a journey that requires us to trek uphill. The path before us is muddied with emotions. We have to navigate around patches of thorns that represent heartache and climb over boulders that are obstacles to following God. The route that was once so clear and easy to negotiate no longer is. And in our confusion, we give up. In our frustration, we walk away. So what a blessing to have a wise and compassionate Shepherd who straightens and levels the road ahead. As we pray for direction, God will lead. He'll show us where to step next. We'll be safe as He guides us through to the end. Let Him direct you in the pathways of His pleasure so nothing can stop you.

Father in heaven, I will look to You for guidance as I walk the pathway of righteousness. Smooth out the path ahead, but even more, be with me. Bless me with Your presence, which brings peace and comfort to my heart. In the name of Jesus I pray. Amen.

NOT IMPOSSIBLE

"Not one promise from God is empty of power.
Nothing is impossible with God!"
LUKE 1:37 TPT

This short scripture is packed with truth that offers good news for those who embrace it! Too often, we feel hopeless. We're certain there's no way that what we desperately need to happen will happen. And so rather than ask for a second opinion on a test result, we become fatalistic. We give up. We walk away from a challenging relationship because it's too difficult. We throw in the towel on becoming pregnant and fall into a depression. We decide we'll always be single, so we begin to shy away from community. Sometimes we decide God isn't for us. We think He may be angry or unhappy with things we've done. And when we get to the end of our strength, we wave the white flag in defeat. Let's be women who dig deeper into our faith when things begin to feel impossible. Let's remember that God's promises are never empty of power. And instead of despairing when we feel we're hitting a wall, let's choose to trust the Lord for answers and possibilities.

Father in heaven, bless me with the kind of faith that doesn't waver in belief. Strengthen me so I am able to trust that You are with me and for me always. Deposit in me the steadfast truth that nothing is impossible with You! In the name of Jesus I pray. Amen.

HIS CANOPY OF KINDNESS AND JOY

Lord, how wonderfully you bless the righteous.
Your favor wraps around each one and covers
them under your canopy of kindness and joy.
PSALM 5:12 TPT

When we choose a life of faith, we're covered. We're covered by the blood of Jesus. We're sheltered by God's protection. We are shielded by His love and sovereignty. And today's scripture tells us we're also covered by a canopy of kindness and joy. What does that mean? God shows kindness through blessing. He restores marriages. He provides necessary and basic resources. He gives confidence and courage. He gives favor, opening doors at the right time. He blesses with creativity and strategy. And as for joy, have you ever noticed how some are full of praise and expectation even when their lives are a hot mess? In the middle of heartache, it's God who will give us unexplainable joy. Just because your life is falling apart doesn't mean you have to be. And when you ask God to steady and strengthen you for the battle, He will do so. The Lord will bless you in surprising ways, including being covered by His kindness and joy.

Father in heaven, thank You for blessing the ones who purpose to live a life right with You. I'm so grateful You choose to cover me with Your greatness simply because I am Yours. I'm humbled You've chosen me. I love You! In the name of Jesus I pray. Amen.

MAKE THIS YOUR ONE PURPOSE

As for me, the last thing I would ever do is to stop praying for you.
That would be a sin against the Eternal One on my part. I will
always try to teach you to live and act in a way that is good
and proper in His eyes. Make this your one purpose: to revere
Him and serve Him faithfully with complete devotion
because He has done great things for you.

1 SAMUEL 12:23–24 VOICE

Let your one purpose in life be to respect, worship, and serve God. Do so faithfully. Be committed to it every day. Live in a way that will please the Lord, making sure your words and actions reflect your loyalty to Him. But let's be honest. This isn't easy to walk out. It takes sacrifice and focus, as well as daily prayer asking for strength. So, why do it? Life is hard enough, right? Why make it harder? We must pray for a change of mind to realize that making this our one purpose isn't a jail sentence but rather an opportunity to reveal our gratitude. We can show appreciation for the blessings we've experienced at God's hands by focusing on following His will and ways.

Father in heaven, thank You for not expecting perfection from me and for knowing it's not possible even if I tried. May my one purpose be to glorify You in how I choose to live my life. In the name of Jesus I pray. Amen.

HAVING A HEALTHY
SENSE OF VALUE

So be content with who you are, and don't put on airs.
God's strong hand is on you; he'll promote you at the right
time. Live carefree before God; he is most careful with you.

1 Peter 5:6–7 msg

Can we agree it's hard to be content with who we are? We may feel fine in the safety of our own homes, but when we turn on the TV, peruse social media, or subscribe to society's trends, we begin to doubt ourselves. We feel unworthy or unlovable, and it affects intimacy in our relationships, confidence in parenting, bravery in speaking up for truth, and courage to advocate for ourselves. We may even act haughty, trying to cover up the deep disappointment with certain parts of our lives. Listen, friend, God wants you to trust Him enough to be confident. When He created you, it was a process of careful planning. You are exactly as He designed. Ask the Lord to bless you with a healthy sense of value—to see yourself the way He sees you. Let Him align your self-esteem with His truth.

Father in heaven, I'm struggling to embrace how You've made me. I look around at others and it makes me feel inferior. Give me Your perspective of who I am. Help me trust Your creation. And let me accept my perfect imperfections and move on. In the name of Jesus I pray. Amen.

THE BLESSINGS OF TESTS AND TRIALS

And I will put this one-third through the fire—refine them all as silver is refined, test them all as gold is tested. They will invoke My name, trust in My promises, and I will answer them. I will announce, "These are My people"; and they will confess, "The Eternal is our God."

ZECHARIAH 13:9 VOICE

So often, it's the fires of life that God uses to refine us. When faced with trouble, we'll run either to God or away from Him. When we cling to God in those difficult moments, we are refined and made more like Jesus. We may not understand how He can use heartache to purify and perfect us, but He does. God promises to restore us, and chances are we've all seen Him use hardship for good in our lives or someone else's. What did these situations produce? A closer connection with the Lord. Few things can create intimacy better than navigating a fire together. Those are defining moments that bond us to each other. If you see them from a divine perspective, you'll recognize the blessings that come from tests and trials.

Father in heaven, thank You for loving me enough to use everything in my life to make me more like Your Son. I'm in awe of how You use all things together to bring about good. In the name of Jesus I pray. Amen.

TAKING A DECISIVE STAND WITH GOD

*Be well balanced and always alert, because your enemy,
the devil, roams around incessantly, like a roaring lion looking
for its prey to devour. Take a decisive stand against him and
resist his every attack with strong, vigorous faith. For you
know that your believing brothers and sisters around the world
are experiencing the same kinds of troubles you endure.*

1 PETER 5:8–9 TPT

Taking a decisive stand against the Enemy requires a strong, believing faith. We need God's help to resist the attacks that come our way. Our human-sized strength can't help us battle the one who is looking to destroy us. We aren't fast enough, smart enough, or strong enough. But when we ask God for help, we can be well balanced rather than allow our emotions to spiral out of control. He'll give us wisdom and discernment so we can be alert to the situations at hand. We don't need to live in fear, because God is stronger than the Enemy. He's smarter than any plan the devil can devise. And He is our protector. Friend, you're blessed to have a heavenly Father who loves with such ferocity and cares with unmatched intensity.

Father in heaven, stand with me and empower me to take a decisive stand against the Enemy's plans. With Your help, I will not fall prey to them again. In the name of Jesus I pray. Amen.

PROMPTED TO
PRAY FOR OTHERS

Every time I think of you—and I think of you often!—I thank
God for your lives of free and open access to God, given
by Jesus. There's no end to what has happened in you—
it's beyond speech, beyond knowledge. The evidence
of Christ has been clearly verified in your lives.

1 CORINTHIANS 1:4–6 MSG

When God brings people to mind, bless them right then and there by
lifting their names up in prayer. Trust that if the Lord put them on your
heart, it's for a good reason. If you are constantly thinking of someone
and the battle she's traversing, just take her to God's throne room. The
truth is God knows exactly what she's fighting, so you don't have to
have all the details. It's not necessary to know exactly what help she
needs. It doesn't require a phone call for more information. There's no
reason to ignore the prompting because you aren't sure what's going
on. Just be obedient and ask God to meet the pressing needs. Ask Him
to give peace and wisdom. Pray for her faith to increase as she relies
on the Lord. And then thank God for the privilege to approach Him
on her behalf.

Father in heaven, help me notice Your prompting
and immediately pray for the ones You place on my
heart. Let my heart be ready and willing to respond
to Your nudge. In the name of Jesus I pray. Amen.

SUFFERING IS CERTAIN BUT BRIEF

*And then, after your brief suffering, the God of all loving grace,
who has called you to share in his eternal glory in Christ, will
personally and powerfully restore you and make you stronger
than ever. Yes, he will set you firmly in place and build you up.
And he has all the power needed to do this—forever! Amen.*

1 PETER 5:10–11 TPT

What a blessing to realize all suffering will eventually come to an end. Because every one of us will experience hurt and sadness at times in our lives, let it encourage you to remember that suffering will be brief. Pain will happen, but it won't be forever. What's more, scripture says that once the suffering is past, God will personally bring restoration. He will strengthen you. He will build you up as He secures your footing. Thank the Lord for bringing good things from hard things. Tell Him why knowing this truth makes a difference when you're struggling. And when those difficult moments arrive, be quick to pray for help, asking God to give you the faith to weather storms with hope and expectation. He has the power necessary to bring you through safely.

**Father in heaven, give me the right perspective to know what I'm
walking through is temporary. And bless me by bringing beauty
from ashes so my testimony of Your greatness will be powerful
to those who need hope. In the name of Jesus I pray. Amen.**

CHOOSING A RIGHTEOUS LIFE

Walk away from the evil things in the world—just leave them behind,
and do what is right, and always seek peace and pursue it. For the Lord
watches over the righteous, and His ears are attuned to their prayers.
But His face is set against His enemies; He will punish evildoers.
1 PETER 3:11–12 VOICE

To be righteous means to be right with God. It means you are actively pursuing the Lord every day and living in ways that glorify Him. When met with a decision, you choose the right path rather than the easy one. Instead of being satisfied by the things of the world, you walk away and leave them behind. And when things get tough, you surrender control as you wait for the Lord to rectify the situation. Scripture says that living righteously guarantees God's ears will be attuned to your prayers. He is always listening for your voice to rise into the heavens. Friend, there are beautiful blessings that come from choosing His way over the world's way. Ask Him to help you choose well.

Father in heaven, my heart's desire is to live a life that not only glorifies You but also makes me more like Your Son. I know purposeful living will be blessed by You. So help me walk away from the evil in the world and embrace all the Christian life offers. In the name of Jesus I pray. Amen.

BLESSINGS ATTACHED

Finally, all of you, be like-minded and show sympathy, love, compassion, and humility to and for each other—not paying back evil with evil or insult with insult, but repaying the bad with a blessing. It was this you were called to do, so that you might inherit a blessing.
1 PETER 3:8–9 VOICE

Ask God to help you be the kind of woman who is full of compassion and love for others, even when they seem undeserving. Ask Him to birth humility in you so you're selfless rather than selfish. Pray for a heavenly perspective so you don't live with a vengeful ideology but instead treat those around you with kindness regardless of how they treat you. This is who you were created to be. When you ask God for His help to walk this out, you will receive it; the reality is we all need His strength and vision. What's more, there's a blessing attached to living with this intentionality. It could be a long life, strong community bonds, a fulfilling marriage, good health, or something else altogether. And while we don't follow God's will and ways simply for the benefits and blessings, we can certainly appreciate them nonetheless.

Father in heaven, I want to live in such a way that I bless You and those around me. Give me the ability to live out today's scripture in my everyday life. In the name of Jesus I pray. Amen.

WHEN YOU NEED HIS COVERING

*When you abide under the shadow of Shaddai, you are hidden in
the strength of God Most High. He's the hope that holds me and the
stronghold to shelter me, the only God for me, and my great confidence.*

PSALM 91:1–2 TPT

The psalmist used some very powerful words in today's scripture: *abide*,
hidden, *shelter*. They each indicate a desire or a need to be covered.
Can you remember a time these words were exactly what you needed?
Maybe your reputation was under fire because of gossip going around.
Maybe your angry overreaction caused embarrassment. Maybe you
had a moral failure, and it was uncovered. Did your marriage dissolve?
Did the big idea you'd been working so hard on get shot down publicly?
Were you feeling exposed? Friend, God is the hope that will hold you
tight through the storms of life. He's the one who will heal your broken
heart and restore the confidence you once had. Let the Lord be your
strength when you want to hide away. It's God who will bless you with
His peace as you live in His shadow. Let Him be your stronghold.

**Father in heaven, cover me right now. I'm battling deep
insecurity, and You're the one who can save me. Remind
me of who I am in Your eyes. Build my confidence and
courage. And give me perspective to see the truth of
what's happening. In the name of Jesus I pray. Amen.**

HIS ARMS OF FAITHFULNESS

He will rescue you from every hidden trap of the enemy,
and he will protect you from false accusation and any deadly
curse. His massive arms are wrapped around you, protecting
you. You can run under his covering of majesty and hide. His
arms of faithfulness are a shield keeping you from harm.

PSALM 91:3–4 TPT

Have you ever known a fantastic hugger? There's nothing like an embrace from someone bigger who can literally envelop you in their arms. It makes you feel protected, shielded from the dangers of the world. It blots out the light as you hide your face in their chest or shoulder. The tighter the squeeze, the safer you feel. Now imagine what it would feel like having God's massive arms wrapped around you. He has the power to stop every hidden or known trap from coming to fruition. He trumps anything the Enemy has planned. So when you're afraid or anxious, you can run into His arms of faithfulness, and He will take care of you. You set that in motion by going to Him in prayer and asking for help. You ask for the blessing of His presence so you can be comforted. And you tell Him how you're feeling and ask for peace.

Father in heaven, I'm running to You right now. You know my fears and worries, and I'm asking You to cover me through this mess. In the name of Jesus I pray. Amen.

ANGELS ON SPECIAL ASSIGNMENT

God sends angels with special orders to protect you wherever
you go, defending you from all harm. If you walk into a trap,
they'll be there for you and keep you from stumbling.
PSALM 91:11–12 TPT

We are blessed to have angels on special assignment to travel with us as we come and go. We can't see them with our eyes, but they are there defending us as ordered by God Himself. Look at all the trouble we have gotten ourselves into as well as the times we've experienced trauma, and consider how often angels must have saved us from things much worse. They've been shielding us from the Enemy's plans for discouragement and destruction in every area of our lives. And they take their job very seriously. Oh how God loves us to provide 24-7 protection! What's more, since we know God is sovereign, any trouble that came into our lives had His approval first. He chose to allow it for our benefit and His glory. Take a moment to thank the Lord for thinking of everything!

Father in heaven, what a privilege to have angels You handpicked to keep me safe. How amazing to know You care so much and make good on Your promise to always protect me. It makes me feel significant and valued, and I'm so grateful You love me so. In the name of Jesus I pray. Amen.

GOD WANTS A RELATIONSHIP

For here is what the Lord has spoken to me: "Because you loved me, delighted in me, and have been loyal to my name, I will greatly protect you. I will answer your cry for help every time you pray, and you will feel my presence in your time of trouble. I will deliver you and bring you honor."

PSALM 91:14–15 TPT

Did you notice the connection in these verses? A relationship takes two to make it beautiful and beneficial. Each person contributes to make it wonderful. This also applies to our relationship with the Lord. In His kindness and generosity, we're blessed! God promises to protect us. He guarantees to answer our cries and pleas for help every time we pray. He pledges we'll feel His presence when struggling. God vows to deliver us and bring honor. And what is our part? We're to love the Lord and delight in Him. We're to be faithful and loyal to Him. This isn't a call to perform to get God to act; He has chosen to love us without condition. But He does want a relationship with us. And that means both sides see value and act accordingly.

Father in heaven, I want to grow in my relationship with You because of who You are and not what You can do for me. Thank You for the blessing of loving me unconditionally. I won't take that for granted. In the name of Jesus I pray. Amen.

WE NEED GOD IN
EVERY SEASON

*GOD, my shepherd! I don't need a thing. You have bedded
me down in lush meadows, you find me quiet pools
to drink from. True to your word, you let me catch
my breath and send me in the right direction.*

PSALM 23:1–3 MSG

So often, we find ourselves clinging to God in the tough seasons of life. We hold on to Him with all we've got because we are scared and worried and unsure of the future. In our insecurity, we draw so close because we recognize He is our only hope. Many times, our faith is never stronger than when we are in a messy situation. It's the times we aren't desperate and don't need anything that we struggle to stay connected. We're in a good place with our relationships. Our health and finances are stellar, and our work and home life are rockin' it. That's when we forget our constant need for God. Be careful, friend. Be mindful that the lush meadows and quiet pools are an oasis. Be present with Him in these times too. These are blessed moments to catch our breath and regroup before we continue on. And our relationship with God is just as valuable in these times as in the battle.

**Father in heaven, thank You for reminding me to
stay present with You. You bless me in every season
of life. In the name of Jesus I pray. Amen.**

THE GOD OF THE DARK VALLEY

Even when the way goes through Death Valley, I'm not afraid when you walk at my side. Your trusty shepherd's crook makes me feel secure.

PSALM 23:4 MSG

What dark valley are you walking through right now, friend? Are you grieving the sudden loss of a family member? Are you weary from years of trying to get pregnant with no positive result? Did you discover the secret life your husband was leading—one full of betrayal? Were you the victim of a crime? Are you working through trauma? Are you unable to find meaningful employment? Has a person of trust turned their back on you? There is no shortage of painful situations and circumstances. But God promises to walk through each valley with us. He will be right there, guiding us through every step. The Lord is our Shepherd, and He knows the way back to the light. So grab hold of God's mighty hand and feel safe in His protection. Ask Him to calm your anxiety and fear so you can walk in faith. You will be blessed as you trust His lead.

Father in heaven, in those dark-valley moments, remind me I can take Your hand whenever I need it. I know You will lead me through each valley unscathed. Give me confidence and courage to ask You for help rather than try to go it alone. In the name of Jesus I pray. Amen.

LET GOD EXACT VENGEANCE

You serve me a six-course dinner right in front
of my enemies. You revive my drooping head;
my cup brims with blessing.

PSALM 23:5 MSG

Life isn't fair, is it? It often feels as if evil wins more times than not. Bad people seem to get away with so much and rarely pay a price. In many cases, the truth is trumped by lies. And what's good is seen as wrong, and what's wrong is seen as good. The Enemy may have dominion over the world, but you are not of the world. Your life here isn't promised to be easy or painless, but that doesn't give you a free pass for payback. Instead, the Lord wants you to live in such a way that your words and actions point to Him. This is a call to rise above the negativity in life and let God be the one to exact vengeance. It's not your job. And when you take on the role of judge and jury, it often leads down the path of sin. Today's verse says that God serves us a six-course meal while our enemies watch. We receive His goodness while they only observe. They're not invited to the table. When you feel the itch for retaliation, pray for a reminder of this banquet image. In the end, you'll receive the blessings. Not them.

Father in heaven, You're judge and jury.
Not me. In the name of Jesus I pray. Amen.

CHASED BY GOD'S LOVE

Your beauty and love chase after me every day of my life.
I'm back home in the house of GOD for the rest of my life.
PSALM 23:6 MSG

God's love is chasing after you right now. Even when you turn your back on the Lord, He pursues with passion. When you reach for the offerings of the world for comfort instead of God, He is still persistent to follow you. Your anger doesn't stop Him. The blame game you often play with Him doesn't negate His pursuit. Any momentary lapse of reason that may drive you from God never tempts Him to walk away. You are deeply loved, constantly cared for, and forever valued by Him. As you allow that truth to sink in, open your heart to receive everything He has for you. Stop running, and embrace the love God wants to pour out. He is the one who will calm your anxious heart and help you find your footing once again. So choose today to grab on to His steadfast compassion and grace. Everything about God is a blessing.

Father in heaven, forgive me for the times I've closed my heart to You. In my pain, I often shut myself off from others as protection. I am beginning to understand the love You have for me, and I want to embrace it with gusto. Let me accept it with gratitude. I need You. In the name of Jesus I pray. Amen.

GOD IS NEVER LATE

He caught Peter and imprisoned him, assigning four squads of soldiers to guard him. He planned to bring him to trial publicly after the Passover holiday. During Peter's imprisonment, the church prayed constantly and intensely to God for his safety. Their prayers were not answered, until the night before Peter's execution.

ACTS 12:4–6 VOICE

Sometimes it's frustrating to wait for God to move on our behalf. There are situations that feel dire, and we are desperate for quick answers. We crave speedy responses to the prayers we pray—but to no avail. Feeling unheard can lead to deep frustration. We can't understand why God doesn't intervene, especially because we live our lives for Him. He could change everything with the snap of His holy fingers. We wonder why God waits as we watch our circumstances deteriorate. It can feel hopeless. It's important to remember that His ways are not our ways and that we can't understand why He works as He does. Honestly, we may never know the why. But the truth remains that God is never late; His timing is perfect. We will be blessed when we choose to trust Him no matter what.

Father in heaven, settle my heart. I've been trying to figure You out, but my job is to activate my faith so I can rest knowing You're in charge. I know Your heart for me is good. In the name of Jesus I pray. Amen.

WHERE DO YOU LOOK FOR HOPE?

I look up to the mountains and hills, longing for God's help.
But then I realize that our true help and protection is only from
the Lord, our Creator who made the heavens and the earth.

PSALM 121:1–2 TPT

Where do you look for help? Who do you count on to save you? Maybe it's a parent who always comes to your financial rescue. It could be a friend who often has the right words to calm you down. Is it a husband or boyfriend who offers a different and welcomed perspective? Maybe you count on the government to create laws and policies that will settle the chaos in your heart. Do you look to the medical community to solve problems? Do you trust the educational system to bring clarity? Or maybe it's yourself. Maybe you begin to manage everyone and everything in hopes that it will bring comfort, hope, and healing. But, friend, God is your true help and protection. He will bless you with understanding. He will keep you safe. He will bring restoration and revitalization. At any time and in every situation, pray to the Lord and let Him be your helper.

Father in heaven, I confess I've looked in too many wrong places for help and hope. Forgive me. Today, moving forward, I will look only to You. All of my needs will be met because of Your goodness and sovereignty. In the name of Jesus I pray. Amen.

IN THE NIGHTTIME HOURS

He will guard and guide me, never letting me stumble or fall.
God is my keeper; he will never forget nor ignore me. He will never
slumber nor sleep; he is the Guardian-God for his people, Israel.

PSALM 121:3–4 TPT

You can talk to God anytime of the day or night because He never
sleeps. Be it a quick prayer or one with lots of detail and emotion, the
Lord is listening. And it's in those nighttime hours we often need God's
ear the most. When it's dark and quiet, our thoughts often run wild,
filling our minds with horrible outcomes and endings. That's when we
desperately need to talk to the one who can bring peace and comfort.
So, friend, what is it that keeps you up at night? Are you worried about
a hard conversation you need to have? Are you feeling overwhelmed by
your schedule? Is the devastating fight with your loved one on replay?
Are the bills more than you can pay? Are your symptoms increasing?
God stands guard over you. He will guide you through the mess so you
don't fall. Trust you're not forgotten. Let the Lord be your confidant,
and be blessed by it.

Father in heaven, hear my voice and help me.
I'm in uncharted waters, and I'm worried about my
circumstances. Show me the way through to the other
side. I trust You. In the name of Jesus I pray. Amen.

HE IS YOUR PROTECTOR

He's protecting you from all danger both day and night. He will keep you from every form of evil or calamity as he continuously watches over you. You will be guarded by God himself. You will be safe when you leave your home, and safely you will return. He will protect you now, and he'll protect you forevermore!

PSALM 121:6–8 TPT

One of the most amazing promises God offers us is protection. With Him, we are safe and sound. And while that doesn't mean we won't ever face hard times or scary situations, it does mean He will be with us every step of the way. Through His Holy Spirit, God will infuse us with power so we're able to navigate the tricks and turns life brings our way. He will bless you with His presence, standing watch over you day and night. As you leave home and return, the Lord will keep you covered by His love. His eyes will be on you always and forever, so nothing will catch Him off guard. Think about it. The Creator of the world is protecting you. Whoa. What a blessing to recognize this powerful truth. When you're in a right relationship with God, your prayers for help won't go unanswered.

Father in heaven, that You would be so interested in my protection is a blessing. I love You and am humbled by the intensity of Your compassion. In the name of Jesus I pray. Amen.

BLESSED WHEN YOU TRUST

"But blessed is the man who trusts me, GOD, the woman who sticks with GOD. They're like trees replanted in Eden, putting down roots near the rivers—never a worry through the hottest of summers, never dropping a leaf, serene and calm through droughts, bearing fresh fruit every season."
JEREMIAH 17:7–8 MSG

Think about how wonderful it feels to jump in a pool after a day in the blazing-hot sun. When you're dripping with sweat from a day of yard work, a cold shower can rejuvenate your body and mind. How refreshing it is to put your feet in a cool stream after a strenuous hike—it has the power to recharge you! And dumping a bottle of water over your head after a long run can renew your energy. Each time you place your trust in God to meet you in scary and exhausting circumstances, your faith will be invigorated and energized in the same way. It will revive you so you can continue. You'll be strengthened through His Spirit to stand strong. And when your situation heats up, your faith will let you cool down. God will bless you with peace.

Father in heaven, I'm sticking with You. No matter what, I'm placing my trust in You to restore my weary heart. Let my faith grow and mature, because I can't do this life without You! In the name of Jesus I pray. Amen.

THE END OF THE ROPE

"You're blessed when you're at the end of your rope.
With less of you there is more of God and his rule."

MATTHEW 5:3 MSG

In our human strength, we work to fix things ourselves. We are doers by nature, amen? We sweat over the details as we try to make sense of them. We try to control and manipulate so we can get the outcome we want the most. We walk around stressed out, wringing our hands as we worry. Then we throw our hands in the air in anger, realizing our limitations are real, and it's frustrating. We're at the end of our rope and hanging on for dear life. There is something so beautiful about coming to the end of ourselves. It means we've arrived at the revelation that we don't have what it takes apart from God. Are you there today? If so, scripture says this is a good place to be because less of you means more of Him! So rather than beat yourself up for not being enough, see the blessing of God having more room to work in your life. Sometimes the best thing we can do is get out of the way.

Father in heaven, thank You that I don't have to figure it all out on my own. Help me step aside and let You bring the hope and help I need. In the name of Jesus I pray. Amen.

CONFIDENCE TO BE CONTENT

"You're blessed when you're content with just who you are—
no more, no less. That's the moment you find yourselves
proud owners of everything that can't be bought."
MATTHEW 5:5 MSG

Finding a way to feel good about who you are is a worthy yet difficult pursuit because the world works against us. The world sets standards that are unreachable and unstable—changing as quick as the direction of the wind. We're often left chasing an idea of acceptance that continues to elude us. Friend, we can't win this battle alone. But when we pray for God to give us His eyes so we can see ourselves the way He does, it changes everything. Start asking for the gift of grace so you can learn to accept your flaws and imperfection. Ask for a heart of acceptance. Let God fill you with His perspective so the trends of the world don't become an idol in your heart. And when you find divinely inspired confidence to be content with how God made you, it's worthy of a celebration. It's a blessing from above.

Father in heaven, I confess there are so many times I
struggle to like myself. When I look at what society values,
it trips me up. Help me care more about what You say is
important. Keep my eyes focused on Your will more than
the world's ways. In the name of Jesus I pray. Amen.

FREEDOM FROM HOPELESSNESS

*Out of my deep anguish and pain I prayed, and God, you helped
me as a father. You came to my rescue and broke open the way
into a beautiful and broad place. Now I know, Lord, that you
are for me, and I will never fear what man can do to me.*

PSALM 118:5–6 TPT

Sometimes when we're in deep anguish, agony, or anxiety, we hide
away. The pain and fear are so great that we struggle to function, so
we go into our hidey-hole. We retreat from community and ignore any
help offered. And we sink deeper into our broken heart. Reread today's
passage of scripture, and be encouraged by God's love for you. You
are something special to Him, and the Lord will move mountains to
rescue those who love Him. There's no shame in praying to God when
you're at the end of yourself. You don't have to be in good spirits or
have the perfect words. And you don't have to have everything figured out. As a matter of fact, you can come to God broken and scared.
He will bring you into a spacious place where you'll find freedom
from hopelessness.

**Father in heaven, I'm so grateful You see me in my pain and
anguish. And I'm so thankful You're always there to pull me
from the pit and into broad places. Bless me with freedom
from hopelessness. In the name of Jesus I pray. Amen.**

TRUST IN THE LORD TO SAVE YOU

*Lord, it is so much better to trust in you to save me than to put
my confidence in someone else. Yes, it is so much better to trust in
the Lord to save me than to put my confidence in celebrities.*

PSALM 118:8–9 TPT

It's so easy for us to put our faith in others. We want to trust our parents
to always have our back. We want to know our boyfriend or husband
will be there to pick up the pieces after a hard day. We need to believe
our kids will honor us well into our golden years or we won't feel a
sense of security. We trust our friends to stand with us through the
ups and downs of life. We may trust doctors, governments, systems,
and processes to keep us safe and sound. But if we are depending on
them more than God, we're setting ourselves up for an epic letdown.
Our family and friends may love us and want what's best, but they
aren't our saviors. They may have every good intention, but they're
not almighty. And even if they've always been there, life is unpredict-
able at every turn. Let today's scripture encourage you to place your
trust in God above all others. He alone will save and restore.

**Father in heaven, the blessing of Your presence is where
I put my trust. In the name of Jesus I pray. Amen.**

GOD'S SUPERNATURAL SOLUTIONS

*Yes, they surrounded me, like a swarm of killer bees swirling
around me. I was trapped like one trapped by a raging fire;
I was surrounded with no way out and at the point of collapse.
But by Yahweh's supernatural power, I overcame them all!*

PSALM 118:11–12 TPT

Chances are you can remember a time or two when you felt trapped. Maybe it was a blunt conversation you didn't see coming. Maybe your innocent plans backfired. Maybe it was a hurtful rant from someone unexpected, and you were unable to respond in the moment. Maybe it was a decision the group made, and you were stuck in the middle of a reckless situation. Regardless of whether you or someone else is responsible, no one likes to feel stuck in a situation or surrounded by difficult circumstances. It's claustrophobic for our hearts. But, friend, God is an expert on freedom. He knows exactly how to make us overcomers. And when you pray for the Lord to intervene, He will bless you with supernatural solutions that lead to liberty.

**Father in heaven, I confess the times I've tried to free myself
from the tangles of life. I've worked to loosen the knots
keeping me from peace and joy. But my efforts can't hold a
candle to the blessing of Your supernatural solutions. Thank
You for rescuing me. In the name of Jesus I pray. Amen.**

THE GATEWAY TO GOD

I have found the gateway to God, the pathway to his
presence for all his devoted lovers. I will offer all my
loving praise to you, and I thank you so much for
answering my prayer and bringing me salvation!
PSALM 118:20–21 TPT

When you choose to receive Jesus as your Savior, recognizing He is the Son of God and the one who paid the price for your sins—past, present, future—you have found the gateway to God. Jesus' blood on the cross made you clean in the eyes of the Lord because He now sees you through that cleansing blood. His sacrifice bridged the gap between you and the Father that sin created. So choosing to follow Jesus opens the pathway to His presence in your life. It secures your salvation and your eternal life with the Lord in heaven. And it gives you access to God, drawing on His strength and might. His wisdom and discernment. His joy and peace. His patience and perseverance. His kindness and generosity. And when you pray in earnest according to God's will, He will answer your prayers in beautiful ways. That blessing is worthy of praise!

Father in heaven, I see now how very blessed I am through Jesus' blood. I see the blessing of Your presence in my life, guiding and gifting me. What a privilege to serve You. I love You with all my heart. In the name of Jesus I pray. Amen.

BREAKTHROUGH-VICTORY

O God, please come and save us again;
bring us your breakthrough-victory!
PSALM 118:25 TPT

One of the most beautiful blessings God provides to those who love
Him is saving us when we need it the most. Sometimes we're fully
aware of our desperation for His help because we were the ones who
got ourselves into the mess. Our bad choices landed us right in the
pit. But then there are times we don't have a clue what's around the
corner, and He protects us from it. It's only later we realize the bullet
we dodged. God is a God of breakthrough-victory. He is the one who
straightens the crooked paths we find ourselves on. He brings clarity
into our hearts and minds, equipping us to make the right decisions.
We are blessed by His care of the details in each situation. And His
compassion is expansive, covering every inch of our lives from first
breath to last. If you are desperate for victory over the struggles you're
facing, God is ready to bring it. The world has nothing for you, friend.
Go to the Lord and tell Him what you need.

Father in heaven, I've tried it all. I've looked in all the wrong
places for help. I know You are the answer and have been all
along. Bring Your breakthrough-victory into my life. Bless me
with Your saving grace. In the name of Jesus I pray. Amen.

THANKING GOD ALL THE TIME

So let's keep on giving our thanks to God, for he is so good! His constant, tender love lasts forever!

PSALM 118:29 TPT

There is a powerful significance to thanking God on a continuous basis, so harness the truth in today's verse, and walk it out in your own life. When we take time to recognize the ways He has blessed our relationships, our finances, our health, our parenting. . .we're the ones encouraged. Seeing how God has honored our hopes and dreams and the desires of our hearts, we can't help but be reassured of His goodness. Recognizing our blessings allows us to find the courage to stand strong again. Why? Because it reminds us of His awesome power and wisdom. We are comforted knowing He is sovereign and in full control. It allows us to rest and trust in the one who can bring about change. And since He has blessed us with redemption and restoration in the past, we can exhale knowing He will do it again.

Father in heaven, when I take a moment to think of all the ways You've blessed me just in the past week, I am humbled. You are kind and generous in the ways I need, as well as in unexpected ways I never knew were important. Thank You for seeing me and knowing how to bless me in the right ways and at the right time. In the name of Jesus I pray. Amen.

DELIGHTED BY GOD

What delight comes to the one who follows God's ways!
He won't walk in step with the wicked, nor share the
sinner's way, nor be found sitting in the scorner's seat.
His passion is to remain true to the Word of "I AM,"
meditating day and night on the true revelation of light.

PSALM 1:1–2 TPT

Ask God to give you the kind of passion that allows you to stay true to the Lord. Ask Him to strengthen you to choose His ways over the world's because it's not always an easy decision to make. Ask God to give you a heart of compassion so you can be a lover of people rather than a ridiculer and scoffer. Every morning, pray that He will give you the courage and confidence to remain faithful in all you do. And pray for focus to keep God at the forefront of your mind so you're able to discern right from wrong. This intentional living opens you up for blessings of all kinds. It shows the Lord what's important to you and what you value the most. So enjoy Him, and let God see the delight He brings into your life.

Father in heaven, help me love You with all that I am.
Show me ways to keep You first in my life so I can be
blessed by Your presence every day. You are the delight
of my life! In the name of Jesus I pray. Amen.

BE RESILIENT AND FAITHFUL

He will be standing firm like a flourishing tree planted
by God's design, deeply rooted by the brooks of bliss,
bearing fruit in every season of life. He is never dry,
never fainting, ever blessed, ever prosperous.

PSALM 1:3 TPT

This verse can describe your life if you trust the Lord. He is the one who can help us be resilient and faithful no matter what comes our way. But it's a choice. And it requires prayer. Imagine how your heart would be encouraged if you're in a tough situation and you're able to stand firm and not cower. When the health report is concerning or you default on a loan, your deep roots of faith hold you steady. When you discover the betrayal of someone you trusted, your anchored faith keeps you from being washed away. Regardless of the trials and tribulations, you will be a fruit bearer for the kingdom because God has planted you in the right places. Stay connected to God through prayer and be filled, be strong, be thriving, and be blessed.

Father in heaven, I know that when I stay focused on You, I can weather any storm that comes my way. Faith is what deepens my roots and keeps me upright in the hardest of times. And even when everything crumbles around me, with Your help I can bear fruit to glorify the kingdom. In the name of Jesus I pray. Amen.

GUARDING THE WORD OF GOD

*Jesus commented, "Even more blessed are those who
hear God's Word and guard it with their lives!"*

LUKE 11:28 MSG

God's Word is special and important. It's a living document that has power and truth in its pages. And it offers guidance and direction for every area of life. Too often, though, we take matters into our own hands. We trust in our own strength and wisdom. We lean on our own understanding. We decide we know what's best. But we're called blessed when we hear and read God's Word and we take it to heart. Letting it sink into the marrow of our bones allows us to embrace the authority it gives us through the name of Jesus. Scripture says we must guard it with our lives! We do this by meditating on certain scriptures that empower us to stand strong. We may set aside time each day to watch sermons online or dig into a Bible study. Some may memorize verses weekly. And we can ask God to bring His Word to life in us, letting us see scripture in action as we navigate difficult situations. Regardless of the how, the reality is we'll be blessed when we make God's Word a priority.

**Father in heaven, thank You for Your Word. I know it's
a blessing and an invaluable tool as I walk out faith
every day. In the name of Jesus I pray. Amen.**

THE BLESSING OF ADMITTING SIN

When I finally saw my own lies, I owned up to my sins
before You, and I did not try to hide my evil deeds from
You. I said to myself, "I'll admit all my sins to the Eternal,"
and You lifted and carried away the guilt of my sin.

PSALM 32:5 VOICE

Sometimes we sin and don't even realize we're doing it. It's not malicious or deliberate disobedience, but it's sin nonetheless. Maybe it concerns our thought life or the shows we're binge-watching. Maybe it's an addiction or an idol. Or maybe we know we're sinning but don't think anyone—including God—knows it or sees it. We hide it out of embarrassment. Let's remember that the Lord is our safe place. We can bare our souls before Him and share every detail of our sin with Him. He knows it all anyway! And when we admit our shortcomings, confess our iniquities, the guilt and shame that often accompany them will be removed. It's a blessing that we can be real with God, knowing He won't turn away in disgust or walk away.

Father in heaven, thank You for promising to lift the guilt and shame I've been carrying. Thank You that I can share honestly with You about my sins. And thank You for looking at me through the lens of Jesus' blood rather than the wretchedness of my failures. In the name of Jesus I pray. Amen.

LOVE DEMONSTRATED

"For here is the way God loved the world—he gave his only, unique Son as a gift. So now everyone who believes in him will never perish but experience everlasting life."

JOHN 3:16 TPT

How do you show others love? Are you their source of encouragement? Do you lavish them with gifts? Maybe you give your time, being present in their lives on a regular basis. Maybe you help them navigate difficult situations and challenging seasons of life. Maybe you're a financial resource or a caretaker. Maybe you're a single mom working several jobs to keep your family afloat. Maybe you're a prayer warrior. The truth is, when we love someone, we can't help but demonstrate it through actions. We want others to see our love in action. In the same vein, God showed us His love by sending His Son into our world to pay the price for our sin. He knew we were incapable of making things right on our own, and the Lord's immeasurable love required unmatched sacrifice. The result is the blessing of eternal life for those who love Him. Have you told God what that means to you?

Father in heaven, the idea of being separated from You for eternity is heartbreaking. I realize the only way to secure salvation is through Your Son. Thank You for caring so much, and I thank Jesus for being willing to pay the price. In His name I pray. Amen.

LOOKING AT GOD INSTEAD

But those who set their gaze deeply into the perfecting law of liberty are fascinated by and respond to the truth they hear and are strengthened by it—they experience God's blessing in all that they do!

JAMES 1:25 TPT

God's truth has a powerful way of strengthening us in our weakest moments. When we're battling insecurity or fear or worried about our circumstances, setting our gaze on the promises of God will encourage our hearts and bring hope for the future. Honestly, sometimes it's hard to force our eyes to focus on God, especially when we are full of anxiety. We get locked into staring at what scares us. We obsess over details that overwhelm us. And we ignore the freedom He offers, choosing to stay tangled instead. Ask God to bless you with the confidence necessary to put your trust in Him. Ask for a deeper understanding of the beautiful freedom you can have when you go all in with your faith. And pray that God will untangle any knot that's keeping you from embracing everything your relationship with Him offers.

Father in heaven, help me focus my eyes on You over everything else. Let me crave freedom from what binds me here on earth. And let me be strengthened by Your truths and blessed as I choose to follow the path You have laid out for me. I need Your help to live and love well. In the name of Jesus I pray. Amen.

HE CAME TO MAKE THINGS RIGHT

We need to recognize the reason Jesus came to earth. Once we do, it sets our hearts right and brings a deeper understanding of His love. Think of the sacrifice God made because we matter to Him. Think of what Jesus endured to bridge the gap sin left. Scripture reminds us that He didn't come down here just to make us feel bad. Instead, He came with a grand purpose to right what had gone wrong. God commissioned Jesus because of His compassion for us. The thought of eternity without His beloved was unimaginable, so He made a way for us to be made right in His eyes. He blessed us! Let that sink in, then say a prayer of thanksgiving. Let Him hear your heart of gratitude for His great love and provision.

Father in heaven, my heart is so moved at the blessing of salvation. Forgive me for not taking the time to fully understand the gift of Jesus. It's hard for me to recognize everything that comes with His sacrifice, but I give You my heart of gratitude, hoping it delights You. I'm blessed by knowing I will be with You forever. In the name of Jesus I pray. Amen.

YOU ARE WHO YOU HANG OUT WITH

If you want to grow in wisdom, spend time with the wise. Walk with the wicked and you'll eventually become just like them. Calamity chases the sin-chaser, but prosperity pursues the God-lover.

PROVERBS 13:20–21 TPT

It really does matter what people you choose to surround yourself with. It's important to be thoughtful when immersing yourself in community because you are who you spend time with. You will naturally pick up the characteristics and mindset of the ones you spend the most time with. So if you want to grow in wisdom, spend time with the wise. If you want to grow in your faith, spend time with the faithful. If you want to grow in endurance, spend time with those who have endured a great deal. Surround yourself with people who pursue peace and joy. Hang out with the ones who extend grace and have a heart of compassion. Find lovers of the Lord, and let them be important people in your life. Friend, ask God to bring the right friends into your life, and watch the Lord bless you through the company you keep.

Father in heaven, give me discernment so I am intentional about my community. I know the value of keeping company with those who will encourage and challenge in all the right ways. Bless me with beautiful friendships that last a lifetime and always point to You. In the name of Jesus I pray. Amen.

WHEN WE NEED SAVING

Give thanks to GOD—he is good and his love never quits. Say,
"Save us, Savior God, round us up and get us out of these godless
places, so we can give thanks to your holy Name, and bask in your
life of praise." Blessed be GOD, the God of Israel, from everlasting to
everlasting. Then everybody said, "Yes! Amen!" and "Praise GOD!"

1 CHRONICLES 16:34–36 MSG

Sometimes we need saving. We need rescuing from our circumstances. And there are times God is the only one who can pull us up as we're sinking. Maybe you're reeling from discovering that your husband's private life has been riddled with betrayal. Maybe you discovered the inappropriate things your child has been doing behind your back. Maybe you're a single mom trying to hold everything and everyone together. Maybe you are beginning to see your parents' health fail. Maybe life has exhausted you, and you're feeling weary. Friend, grab on to God and don't let go. He will bless you with strength, wisdom, endurance, and peace. The Lord will guide you through the messiness of life and into a safe space. And in the end, you will stand strong and thank God for saving you.

Father in heaven, hear my cry right now. See my burdened heart.
Step down and pull me from the waters that surround me. I
am desperate to be saved. In the name of Jesus I pray. Amen.

WHEN YOU NEED A REMINDER

The Eternal One bless and keep you. May He make His face
shine upon you and be gracious to you. The Eternal lift up
His countenance to look upon you and give you peace.
NUMBERS 6:24–26 VOICE

Everything about this scripture is a blessing. It's one of those passages that can bring tears to your eyes because you feel the weight of it. You see its importance. You feel the unconditional love. And it fills your heart with gratitude because it speaks right into those places of insecurity that say you are not enough. Today's scripture has the power to make you feel significant and valued. As you reread it, what stands out to you the most? What connects with your weary heart? What brings encouragement? Let this be one of those verses you choose to memorize. Speak it over yourself anytime you're battling a sense of worthlessness. When you need a reminder that God cares, repeat it out loud so you can hear it. God has a lot to say to you through these words, and it will bless you to take them to heart.

Father in heaven, these three verses bring me to tears because they're not something I hear from anybody. I don't always feel loved or seen or known. I don't feel significant or important. But I know You're speaking directly to me through these words, and I need Your help to receive them. In the name of Jesus I pray. Amen.

SAVED BY GRACE

For it's by God's grace that you have been saved. You receive it through faith. It was not our plan or our effort. It is God's gift, pure and simple. You didn't earn it, not one of us did, so don't go around bragging that you must have done something amazing.
EPHESIANS 2:8–9 VOICE

What a blessing to realize we are unable to save ourselves by working hard. It doesn't matter how many hours you volunteer at the shelter. It doesn't matter how much money you donate to charity. It doesn't matter how many homeless people you feed in your community or the number of malaria prevention pills you provide for those living in Africa. You could attend church twice a week, lead a small group, sing in the choir, or rock babies in the nursery, but these things can't buy your salvation. Nothing you do makes it so. It is by faith alone that we are saved. We can't earn it. We can't buy it. We don't deserve it. God's grace has been extended to us through His Son, Jesus, and we're the ones to receive the blessing of eternal life. Thank Him right now.

Father in heaven, I am overwhelmed by Your kindness and generosity. I am deeply moved by the sacrifice of Your Son. And I am grateful my salvation doesn't hinge on anything I can do. In the name of Jesus I pray. Amen.

HEARING GOD'S VOICE

*"My own sheep will hear my voice and I know each one,
and they will follow me. I give to them the gift of
eternal life and they will never be lost and no one has
the power to snatch them out of my hands."*

JOHN 10:27–28 TPT

Because scripture says the Lord's sheep will hear His voice and follow Him, it means we have the capacity to identify God's voice in our lives. It may not be audible, but it's still recognizable. Some people hear through the Bible. They may have read a verse a hundred times, but this one time it lands differently in their spirit. It feels highlighted specifically for them in their situation. Some people have a gut feeling they can't shake, believing it is the Holy Spirit speaking. Others may feel a connection with God in nature by taking in a beautiful sunset, hiking tall mountains, or sitting on the beach staring at the ocean. Everyone has a way special to them. If you are unsure, ask God to bless you with the eyes to see Him and the ears to hear Him. Tell the Lord your desire to know His voice. Ask Him to make it more prominent than the noise that comes from the world so you can recognize it.

**Father in heaven, give me keen discernment to hear
Your voice above all others. And give me the courage
to listen. In the name of Jesus I pray. Amen.**

PLANNED IN ADVANCE

We have become his poetry, a re-created people that will fulfill
the destiny he has given each of us, for we are joined to Jesus,
the Anointed One. Even before we were born, God planned in
advance our destiny and the good works we would do to fulfill it!
EPHESIANS 2:10 TPT

God thought you up, and His creation was magical. He planned out what you would look like, the talents you'd possess, where you would live, the community who would surround you, and when you would come on the world scene. He thought through every detail that makes you, well, you, and He strung them together beautifully. In His deep love, God chose you to be His, joining you with Jesus, His one and only Son. Friend, scripture says you are His poetry! And while sometimes you might feel lost, not knowing your purpose in life, recognize that your destiny and future good works were planned in advance. The Lord considered and confirmed everything before you even took your first breath on planet Earth. That means you are not a mistake. You were planned. You are an intentional creation.

Father in heaven, I'm humbled to think You put so much time and effort into making me who I am. Forgive me for the times I struggle to like myself. And help me be confident so I can do the good works You have planned for me. In the name of Jesus I pray. Amen.

THE GOOD SHEPHERD

*"I alone am the Good Shepherd, and I know those whose
hearts are mine, for they recognize me and know me,
just as my Father knows my heart and I know my Father's
heart. I am ready to give my life for the sheep."*

JOHN 10:14–15 TPT

When you make the decision to follow the Lord, He knows you. When your heart is turned toward Him, you're His forever. In that deciding moment when you accept Jesus as your personal Savior, acknowledging He is the one and only Son of God who died on the cross to pay the price for your sins, He becomes your Shepherd. He is a jealous God who wants to be the only one you look to for hope and help. But too often, we look other places. We look to people who we hope can save us. We look to organizations and corporations. We look to our doctors, first responders, and government officials. We look to what the world can offer. And when we do, we miss the blessing of the Good Shepherd who is ready and able to help us navigate anything life throws our way.

**Father in heaven, please come into my life and save me.
I accept Your gift of salvation through Jesus. I'm so grateful
You have chosen me to be Yours, and today I choose You
to be my Good Shepherd. Please flood my life with Your
glorious presence. In the name of Jesus I pray. Amen.**

WHY WE CARE FOR THE POOR

Whoever cares for the poor makes a loan to the Eternal;
such kindness will be repaid in full and with interest.
PROVERBS 19:17 VOICE

It is a privilege and a burden to love those in need. When we do, though, it delights the heart of God. He notices our generosity and kindness. As we bless others with our resources, it blesses Him. And that knowledge should bless us. Isn't one of our deepest desires to glorify the Lord with our lives? When we care for the poor—be it the financially poor, confidence poor, bravery poor, health poor, joy poor—it stores up heavenly treasures for us. Every time we choose to stand in the gap for someone who's struggling, it's like making a loan to God. And that loan will be paid in full, with interest, when we see Him face-to-face. Ask God to give you a generous heart so you can love others with purpose. Ask for compassion so you can see the need before you. Tell our gracious God you are ready and willing to take care of those He puts in your path.

Father in heaven, I want my life to make a difference.
I want my life to glorify Your name! Open my eyes so I don't
miss any opportunity to help someone in need. Give me a
heart for the poor. In the name of Jesus I pray. Amen.

THE VALUE OF WISDOM

*Blessings pour over the ones who find wisdom, for they have
obtained living-understanding. As wisdom increases, a great
treasure is imparted, greater than many bars of refined gold.
It is a more valuable commodity than gold and gemstones,
for there is nothing you desire that could compare to her.*

PROVERBS 3:13–15 TPT

Today's verses tell us that wisdom is more of a treasure than countless
bars of gold and gemstones. Its value is unmatched. And when we
look at the state of the world, it's easy to see why having wisdom is so
important. Can we agree it is crazy out there? That's why it's vital we
know what is right and what is wrong. We need to be blessed with a
deeper knowledge of how to navigate the ups and downs we face on
the regular. Without a level of discernment, we'll fall prey to the lies
flying around us every day. And friend, the Bible is where we will find
the wisdom we need to survive in today's times. In its pages, we will
find truth. And as we pray, God will affirm the things we've read and
bring them to life. Let the Word of God bless you as you find wisdom
and discernment for the day.

**Father in heaven, as I open Your Word, open my eyes so
I can learn how to navigate life on earth for my benefit
and Your glory. In the name of Jesus I pray. Amen.**

BUT WE WILL NOT

We are cracked and chipped from our afflictions on all sides,
but we are not crushed by them. We are bewildered at times, but we
do not give in to despair. We are persecuted, but we have not been
abandoned. We have been knocked down, but we are not destroyed.
2 CORINTHIANS 4:8–9 VOICE

There is no doubt life is going to beat you up. Chances are it already has. We are going to face daunting and terrifying times. Our hearts are going to be broken in unexpected ways. There will be unforeseen tragedy that knocks on our door. People will criticize us for not being good enough. We'll be persecuted because we believe in God. We will be knocked to our knees by relational troubles, financial struggles, and health issues. We'll be caught off guard by evil more than once. But when we anchor our faith in God, these experiences will not crush us. We won't give in to despair. We'll know without fail that God hasn't abandoned us to figure things out ourselves. And we will not be destroyed. What a blessing to have a heavenly Father who promises to sustain and restore when the storms of life hit.

Father in heaven, life is hard. Sometimes I battle fear and anxiety at overwhelming levels. Bless me with the reminder that You promised to save me. Knowing that keeps me from falling into despair. In the name of Jesus I pray. Amen.

WHERE WILL YOUR FOCUS BE?

*You see, the short-lived pains of this life are creating for us an
eternal glory that does not compare to anything we know here.
So we do not set our sights on the things we can see with our
eyes. All of that is fleeting; it will eventually fade away. Instead,
we focus on the things we cannot see, which live on and on.*

2 CORINTHIANS 4:17–18 VOICE

When you're facing tough times and difficult moments, what you focus
on matters. And the choice is yours to make. You can focus on the mess
you're in, staring into the face of all the worries and what scares you,
or you can focus on God. You'll fix your gaze either on insecurities or
on God's promises. Your sights will be set on everything that could go
wrong or on the redemption coming your way as you place your faith
in the Lord. It's up to you. Why not plan now what your focus will be
for the next challenge you face? Choose today that you'll focus on God
no matter what comes your way tomorrow, making an intentional plan
to activate your faith over your fear.

**Father in heaven, You are the one who calms the storm that
rages in my heart. You are the one who replaces fear with peace
and sadness with hope. You've blessed me before, and I know
You'll bless me again. In the name of Jesus I pray. Amen.**

BLESSING OTHERS IN NEED

"'When did we see you with no place to stay and invite you in? When did we see you poorly clothed and cover you? When did we see you sick and tenderly care for you, or in prison and visit you?' And the King will answer them, 'Don't you know? When you cared for one of the least of these, my little ones, my true brothers and sisters, you demonstrated love for me.'"

MATTHEW 25:38–40 TPT

When you have the opportunity to bless someone with your time or treasure, don't let it pass you by. Even if no one around you sees your generosity, God always does. And it matters greatly to Him when we care for others and meet their needs with our resources. Scripture even says that when we show that kind of compassion, it's a powerful demonstration of our love for the Lord. When you feel prompted to help, step up. When God highlights someone in particular—from the beggar at the intersection to your coworker—find out what that person needs. Don't worry about the details or what people may think. God will take care of those things. Your job is to be willing to bless those in need.

Father in heaven, open my eyes to see the needs of others. Open my heart to hear Your prompting for me to step up and help. In the name of Jesus I pray. Amen.

THE BLESSING OF RESTORATION

I will restore the captives of My people, Israel. They will rebuild their ruined cities and return to them. They will plant new vineyards and drink wine from them, and they will plant new gardens and eat the food they grow. I will plant them in their own soil, and they will never be uprooted again, for this is the land I have given them.

AMOS 9:14–15 VOICE

In the Bible, there are countless examples and stories of God restoring His people. He restored families, positions, lands, laws, groups, and individuals. He gave new names, drew new borders, created new hope, and gave new promotions. God is in the business of restoration even today! He brings beauty from the ashes in our lives. He can heal marriages and make them stronger. He can reinstate courage and confidence so we can move forward. He can reestablish broken relationships with friends and family. God can rebuild our finances from dust. He can repair our broken hearts. He can bring back the peace and joy that our circumstances have drained. Talk to the Lord with authenticity, sharing the shattered places you want pieced back together. Let Him bless you through restoration.

Father in heaven, thank You for being a God who restores. Thank You for seeing the value in bringing important parts of our lives back from the dead. You bless me in beautiful ways. In the name of Jesus I pray. Amen.

GOD WILL NEVER WALK AWAY

How blessed the man you train, GOD, the woman you instruct in your Word, providing a circle of quiet within the clamor of evil, while a jail is being built for the wicked. GOD will never walk away from his people, never desert his precious people. Rest assured that justice is on its way and every good heart put right.

PSALM 94:12–15 MSG

Chances are you've been rejected or abandoned in your life. Maybe a parent had no choice but to put you into the foster care system. Maybe you lost someone unexpectedly. Maybe a husband walked out on your marriage, or a friend turned her back on you. Maybe a child no longer wants a relationship with you. Life on earth can beat you up, but not God. He never will. There's nothing you can do to make God walk away from you. He's incapable of deserting you because His love won't allow it. Even at your very worst when you're throwing a tantrum, spewing hateful words, or taking out your anger on others, God is right there with you. He's offering hope and help for the weary. Let Him be your safe space—a trusting place to be imperfect and honest.

Father in heaven, I am blessed and grateful for Your steadfastness to the ones who love You. Remind me that Your promise to love me forever is unshakable and nonretractable. In the name of Jesus I pray. Amen.

I WOULD HAVE NEVER MADE IT

Who stood up for me against the wicked? Who took my side against evil workers? If GOD hadn't been there for me, I never would have made it. The minute I said, "I'm slipping, I'm falling," your love, GOD, took hold and held me fast. When I was upset and beside myself, you calmed me down and cheered me up.

PSALM 94:16–19 MSG

Have you ever said the words of the psalmist in the scripture above? *"If God hadn't been there for me, I never would have made it."* This sentence may be a staple in your responses to hard situations. You've probably seen the Lord show up in meaningful and unexpected ways before. What a blessing to have a testimony of His faithfulness! Think back on the times God steadied you when something shook your foundation. Do you remember when a wave of peace washed over you in the middle of the storm or you had a sudden sense of joy overcome you? Keep these memories close because in the future you'll need the encouragement they offer. Never forget the ways God has blessed you and those you love.

Father in heaven, I can remember the times You have helped me when I was slipping and falling—the ways You were there to calm me when I was upset. Thank You for blessing me with Your compassion! In the name of Jesus I pray. Amen.

ONE DAY IS BETTER

For just one day of intimacy with you is like a thousand days of joy rolled into one! I'd rather stand at the threshold in front of the Gate Beautiful, ready to go in and worship my God, than to live my life without you in the most beautiful palace of the wicked.

PSALM 84:10 TPT

When you experience the blessings and beauty of a faithful life, you'll see only one choice when you reach the fork in the road of decisions again. You will be compelled to follow God's way rather than give in to what the world has to offer. And when you ask, He will give you the strength and wisdom to stand up against every temptation. Then you will be able to testify that better is one day with God than thousands standing in the riches and rewards elsewhere. Friend, ask the Lord to make you brave as you refuse to compromise your morals and beliefs. Ask Him to give you discernment to see what is right and what is wrong. And ask for a heart of worship so you can praise God every day for creating ways to have a more intimate relationship with Him.

Father in heaven, Your presence blesses me, and I crave time alone with You! Give me the resolve to always choose You over the world because there is no comparison. Remind me when I need it. In the name of Jesus I pray. Amen.

FAITH ACTIVATES BLESSING

*For the Lord God is brighter than the brilliance of a sunrise!
Wrapping himself around me like a shield, he is so generous with
his gifts of grace and glory. Those who walk along his paths with
integrity will never lack one thing they need, for he provides it all!*

PSALM 84:11 TPT

God blesses us by providing everything we need. Don't miss this powerful takeaway from today's verse, because it's an undeniable truth we need to embrace and absorb as followers. But also notice the qualifier. God is crazy about you and wants to deepen your relationship, and so He incentivizes faithfulness. He sweetens the pot for those who want to follow Him. When we choose to live everyday life full of integrity and intentionality, the floodgates in heaven open up. God richly blesses our obedience, something the Bible talks about countless times throughout its pages. Remember, it's faith that activates His blessing. And once activated, we will feel God's wraparound shield of protection in our lives. We will be receivers of His kindness and generosity. His gifts of grace and glory will fall upon us in powerful ways.

Father in heaven, bless me with the ability to walk in integrity and honor so my life will glorify You. And thank You for making sure my needs are met when I do. I know You bless those who purpose to bless You. In the name of Jesus I pray. Amen.

TREASURING EVERY STEP

How blessed are those who make Your house their home,
who live with You; they are constantly praising You.
[pause] Blessed are those who make You their strength,
for they treasure every step of the journey [to Zion].

PSALM 84:4–5 VOICE

Imagine treasuring every step of your journey, including your life right now. How do you cherish struggles in marriage? How do you adore the difficulties of parenting teenagers or toddlers? How do you value seasons of financial fear? How can you appreciate anxiety from your career or hold dear frustrations in friendship? Well, if we look at today's scripture, it says we can be blessed in these times by making God our strength. We can treasure them because we are walking with God, not alone. It means we lean on Him for hope instead of ourselves. We press into His promises to save and restore. It means we adopt a position of praise, thanking God now for the faithfulness we'll see later. This is how we make Him our home. And when we find the courage and confidence to walk this out every day, the blessings will flow. We will come out as victors.

Father in heaven, bless me with Your strength so I can learn to treasure whatever life brings my way. In the good times or the bad, I know You will be with me. In the name of Jesus I pray. Amen.

DOING RIGHT IN HIS EYES

Keep trusting in the Lord and do what is right in his eyes.
Fix your heart on the promises of God, and you will dwell in
the land, feasting on his faithfulness. Find your delight and true
pleasure in Yahweh, and he will give you what you desire the most.

PSALM 37:3–4 TPT

When you come to a crossroads, choose the path that points to God. That's how you trust Him and do what is right in His eyes. How do you know which way to go? Remember to always choose the path of peace. Don't rush your decision. You can take a minute to pray about it, and you can take the time necessary to hear from Him. How do you know you're hearing God's voice? It may be a gut feeling that's persistent. It may be consistent messages over time from His Word, a sermon, or those you trust. It may even be an open or closed door. But when you fix your heart on God's promise to answer your prayers, you will feast on His faithfulness because He will come through for you. Take a deep breath, and enjoy the adventure that comes from following the Lord. You'll be blessed in the most meaningful ways.

Father in heaven, help me trust You and do what is right in Your eyes. Help me find delight and pleasure in my relationship with You! In the name of Jesus I pray. Amen.

LETTING GOD
DIRECT YOUR LIFE

Give God the right to direct your life, and as you trust him along the way, you'll find he pulled it off perfectly! He will appear as your righteousness, as sure as the dawning of a new day. He will manifest as your justice, as sure and strong as the noonday sun.

PSALM 37:5–6 TPT

Did you notice the huge blessing outlined in today's scripture? It's all about choosing to surrender to the Lord, letting Him direct your life. It's recognizing that He is the only trustworthy option available to you. And it requires you to take a gigantic step back so God can assume His rightful position in the driver's seat of your life. Easy? No. But, friend, when you release control into His capable hands, something amazing happens. You'll discover peace and satisfaction. You will experience hope, maybe for the first time. And while life won't be pain- or problem-free, staying tucked behind the shadow of the Lord will shield you from their damaging effects. You'll have the blessing of His eternal perspective to bring a sense of calm in the chaos.

Father in heaven, I've been in the driver's seat for way too long. I've had a false sense of control. But I realize the truth is I'm only safe when You direct my life. You're the one who is trustworthy. And I now see I'm blessed by it! In the name of Jesus I pray. Amen.

BUT THOSE WHO TRUST IN THE LORD

Stay away from anger and revenge. Keep envy far from you,
for it only leads you into lies. For one day the wicked will be
destroyed, but those who trust in the Lord will inherit the land.

PSALM 37:8–9 TPT

Ask the Lord to give you a greater measure of trust in Him. Ask Him to mature your faith so you understand the value of following His will and ways. Pray for Him to strengthen your resolve, to bless you with wisdom and discernment, and to let you feel His presence guiding you along the path He has planned. When we choose to be consumed by our faith, it keeps us away from living in the flesh, which is riddled with sin. Without God in the forefront of our hearts and minds, we will give in to anger. We will plot revenge. We will be filled with jealousy and envy, always wanting what seems out of reach. Our lips will spew lies as we live in dishonesty. We will battle pride and selfishness. And we will fall prey to every wicked way. However, trusting in the Lord will lead to eternal life. And that's a blessing we never want to miss out on.

Father in heaven, help me trust You more. I want to live my life to glorify You and not my flesh. You are the blessing I long for the most. In the name of Jesus I pray. Amen.

LESS OF YOU, MORE OF HIM

It is much better to have little combined with much of God than to have the fabulous wealth of the wicked and nothing else. For the Lord takes care of all his forgiven ones while the strength of evil men will surely slip away.

PSALM 37:16–17 TPT

We're blessed when God is the bigger part of our lives and we are small. Think about it. God brings perfection, and we bring imperfection. His ways are always good, and ours are often laced with the wrong motives. God brings a wise perspective, and we bring big emotions. He's able to see the big picture, and we only see what we want. God forgives, while we keep score. The point here isn't to make us feel terrible about ourselves but to highlight the truth that we need a Savior. Life is just better when God is in the mix because He fills in the gap humanity leaves. He makes up the difference when we fall short. And there is nothing the world can offer that is better than the Lord. Having less of us and more of God is a beautiful blessing that comes from a life of surrender.

Father in heaven, it is a blessing to know I don't have to have everything figured out. I don't have to perform. Instead I can surrender to Your godship and be blessed. In the name of Jesus I pray. Amen.

HOPE WHEN WE STUMBLE

When Yahweh delights in how you live your life,
he establishes your every step. If they stumble badly they
will still survive, for the Lord lifts them up with his hands.

PSALM 37:23–24 TPT

We're not perfect. We all make mistakes. And honestly, we have no
shot at living flawlessly. God knows it, and so do we. So maybe the
idea is to live with purpose instead. Maybe what's most important
is that we live our lives in such a way that others notice a difference.
Know that God will notice too. The words we use and how we treat
others won't only catch their attention but will catch God's attention.
They will point to God in heaven, and the Lord will be delighted by
our intentionality. And the blessing from living with purpose will
manifest in His rescue. Scripture says that if the righteous stumble,
God will catch us and restore us. He will honor those who love Him
and try to keep His ways. Pray for the Lord to equip you to live your
life to glorify Him.

Father in heaven, I need Your help to live in ways that delight
You. On my own, I'm incapable of glorifying Your name. Fill
my heart with the desire. Equip me so my words and actions
always point to You. And establish my every step so I walk in
Your ways in confidence. In the name of Jesus I pray. Amen.

THE BEST COUNSELORS

The faithful lovers of God will inherit the earth and enjoy every promise of God's care, dwelling in peace forever. God-lovers make the best counselors. Their words possess wisdom and are right and trustworthy. The ways of God are in their hearts and they won't swerve from the paths of steadfast righteousness.

PSALM 37:29–31 TPT

When you make God a priority, it flows into every area of your life. It becomes your operating system and the lens through which you look at life. That's why today's scripture says God-lovers make the best counselors. They're steeped in the Word, which is why their advice is always dripping with wisdom and discernment. You can trust the council of those who are faithful lovers of the Lord. Their words are measured. They gather life experiences with God at the helm and share from those places. And they know His commands and the ways He expects us to live because they study scripture. Ask the Lord to bring women of wisdom into your life. Ask Him to bring those who have God in their hearts and exemplify steadfast righteousness. They will bless you in more ways than you can imagine.

Father in heaven, I'd be so blessed to have meaningful relationships with those who faithfully love You. Open my eyes and my heart to receive new friendships, and grow me so I can be a blessing to others too. In the name of Jesus I pray. Amen.

SCRIPTURE INDEX